FOOD FOR FRIENDS

Pillsbury

Dear Friends,

Having company? Great! Somehow, food just tastes better when we can share it with friends. Whether you prefer inviting just a few guests at a time for casual gatherings or enjoy full-scale formal dinner parties, this book is designed to capture all your entertaining moods.

With sumptuous suggestions for every occasion and budget, there are seasonal suppers, tasty trips to foreign shores, mealtime mates for around-the-clock cuisine and deliciously different ways to celebrate anniversaries, the big game, V.I.P.'s for dinner and cozy evenings by the fire.

And, just a word about hosting. The person who entertains with flair and confidence is usually one who, first of all, enjoys having guests, and secondly, takes time to carefully organize party plans well ahead of the big day. Food is prepared in advance as much as possible, the table is artfully set and unnecessary pots and pans are washed and tucked away so that when the doorbell rings, the guests receive the attention. We hope this book will be a frequent inspiration with its imaginative, professionally-tested recipes and step-by-step instructions to guarantee that the finalé will be grand indeed.

We know that when you entertain, you want everything to be just right, so we have highlighted pointers for perfect parties along with full-color, mouth-watering photographs to give you a preview of just how appealing your "creations" will be.

Only one ingredient is missing – the genuine spirit of gracious hospitality which only you can provide. Add that very special personal touch and we are certain that your entertaining will be more enjoyable and festive than ever before.

The Pillsbury Company

Contents

Publisher: William Edgley
Managing Editor: Christine Fossum
Art Directors: Bob Frink, Nancy Plasko
Copy Editor and Menu Coordinator: Heather
  Randall
Photographers: Jack Revoir, Arnold Dittes
Food Stylists: Donnie Flora, Judy Tills
Home Economists: Verone Smith, Betsy
  Norum, Karen Schiemo, JoAnn Cherry,
  Sandra Engan

Entertaining Tips

Many of us claim we don't "entertain" anymore — we just have a few friends over. True, the formal, sit down, black tie dinner is not as common as it once was, but even when you have the neighbors over for an afternoon barbecue you are entertaining. And this calls for a little advanced planning.

Planning ahead includes deciding what kind of party to have, when to hold it, what to serve and how to get everything done on time.

What Kind of Party

Perhaps your party is to celebrate a special event — your daughter's graduation, grandma's birthday or to toast in the New Year. Or perhaps it's just an excuse to have a relaxing time with good friends. Sometimes you will find yourself entertaining unexpectedly — Aunt Tillie has dropped in for the afternoon, or you decide on the spur of the moment with your co-workers to all meet at your house later in the evening for the televised football game.

The reason you are entertaining will help you make some of your other decisions.

Who to Invite

Especially with impromptu and casual entertaining who to invite has often been decided without much effort on your part — it has already been decided that the office workers are all invited over for the football game; that grandma and grandpa will be coming for Johnny's birthday party.

But sometimes, especially with more formal occasions a little time should be spent on the guest list. First, determine how many people you wish to invite. Consider your house size, budget and preparation time.

If you are planning a small gathering, make sure the group is comfortable together. Consider their interests.

It's best to have more diverse groups when the guest list is large. With larger groups it is fun to mix up your guest list — introduce old friends to new and meet new people yourself.

Inviting your Guests

Extend the invitation by mail or phone. If it is a very formal affair, written or printed invitations are required. When phoning, it is a good idea to call at least a week in advance; even earlier during seasons when more entertaining is done.

When inviting by telephone always talk with the person you're inviting; messages sometimes are confused and misplaced, and it's better not to take the chance. Tell your friend about the occasion and then extend the invitation. Don't approach her by asking what she's doing next Sunday afternoon. Give her the option of replying in a day or two in case there is need to discuss it with her husband. Be sure you tell her as much as you would if you sent a written invitation. When using written invitations, mail at least 2 weeks in advance. Include an "RSVP" if you want to plan around an exact number of guests. Be sure to include your phone number and/or address.

For written invitations, there are commercial cards and notes from which to choose. Often, the card features the special occasion you may be celebrating. Or you may be inspired to design clever invitations of your own. In any case, be sure a mailed invitation includes the following information:

WHO is giving the party.
WHAT kind of party is planned and what to wear if it is especially informal or formal or a costume party.
WHEN will it be held (time and date).
WHERE is it being given (address).
HOW long will it last (if you feel this information is necessary, as for an open house or a cocktail party).
WHY is it being held (is there a special reason or occasion that your guests would want to know about — for example, a guest of honor, a birthday or an anniversary).

What to Serve

This is probably the most frustrating problem to the host or hostess but this is actually what our book is all about. Look the chapters over carefully. Think about why you are entertaining. The type of party will often determine to a large extent the foods you will wish to serve. A larger open house cocktail party will call for finger foods so that people can eat and mingle to their satisfaction. At sit down affairs more complicated main dishes and meats may be served.

Although we are excited about each of our menus, they are designed to be flexible. Feel free to mix and match to meet specific needs and tastes, especially within chapters. Do be careful though to note the number of people each recipe serves, you don't want to overflow or worse yet, run short.

The time of day and year, your budget, time you have to shop and prepare for it and type of serving dishes or utensils available are also things to consider.

If you have a freezer you can make a lot of party foods up to a few weeks ahead. This book includes many "make ahead" recipes. They are designed to help you be organized and relaxed at party time.

Menus are more than just food. They should please the eye as well as the palate. They provide contrast in flavor, color and texture. Don't worry if you don't have just the serving dish you saw in the picture. The food will taste just as good out of your serving dishes. If a special dish or utensil is needed, the recipe will say so.

Garnishes add the finishing touch and that extra spark of color which will make any dish look special. If you are shopping anyway, pick up a bunch of parsley, a lemon or two and a sprig of mint. You'll be surprised what they'll do for "picture appeal".

Breakfasts & Brunches

No wonder early-bird entertaining has become so popular in recent years. Just think of the appetizing array of foods one can serve for breakfasts and brunches. And what a gracious way to say "Good Morning" to special friends while offering a pleasant change of pace from the dinner party routine. Use your imagination for this flexible type of gathering and charm everyone with a buffet set up in your country kitchen or little tables arranged in your yard or on the patio for the first al fresco meal of the season. Breakfasts can, of course, begin quite early, but brunches are usually served from midmorning up until about 1 p.m. If the brunch is to be on Sunday, it is a thoughtful hostess who plans her timing to accommodate churchgoers.

Strawberries in sparkling champagne set the stage for a simply spectacular midday feast. With the crêpes prepared and filled before guests arrive, the party becomes as worry-free as it is glamorous. The menu calls for an elegant table and your prettiest accessories because you will want to serve these recipes for the most sparkling occasions — a wedding breakfast, an anniversary brunch or a graduation gala. It is gourmet with a capital "G"!

Champagne Celebration
Sparkling Strawberries
Gourmet Asparagus Crêpes
Fruit Kabobs with
Orange-Ginger Dressing

If fresh strawberries are unavailable, substitute whole frozen berries, slightly thawed and drained.

SPARKLING STRAWBERRIES
    1 pint fresh strawberries, washed and hulled
    ⁴/₅ quart (3¼ cups) champagne or sparkling Burgundy, chilled

Spoon berries into six wine, champagne or sherbet glasses. Chill. Just before serving, pour champagne over the strawberries. Eat the berries with a spoon; then drink the wine from the glass.

6 servings

FRUIT KABOBS WITH ORANGE-GINGER DRESSING
    1 banana, cut into thick slices
    ¼ cup lemon juice
    1 cup pineapple chunks, drained
    1 cup cantaloupe balls
    1 cup honeydew melon balls
    1 cup fresh grapes

Dressing
    8-oz. pkg. cream cheese, softened
    1 tablespoon sugar
    1 tablespoon grated orange peel
    ½ to 1 teaspoon ground ginger
    6 tablespoons orange juice

Dip banana slices in lemon juice to prevent browning. Alternate fruits on 12 bamboo skewers. Chill. In small bowl, blend cream cheese until smooth and creamy. Stir in remaining Dressing ingredients. Chill until serving time. To serve, spoon Dressing over kabobs.

6 servings

Fruit Kabobs with Orange-Ginger Dressing
Gourmet Asparagus Crêpes
Sparkling Strawberries

These delicate crêpes bake to perfection under a creamy mushroom sauce.

GOURMET ASPARAGUS CRÊPES

  1 cup milk
  2 tablespoons cooking oil
  2 eggs
  ½ cup Pillsbury's Best All Purpose or Unbleached Flour
  1 teaspoon baking powder
  ½ teaspoon salt
  8 thin slices (4 oz.) boiled ham
  6 large slices natural Swiss cheese, cut in half
  15-oz. can extra-long green asparagus spears, drained

Mushroom Sauce

  2 jars (2½ oz. each) sliced mushrooms, drained
  3 tablespoons butter or margarine
  3 tablespoons flour
  1 cup water
  2 teaspoons instant chicken bouillon
  ⅓ cup light cream
  ¼ cup (1 oz.) shredded Cheddar cheese
  1 tablespoon chopped chives

In small bowl, beat milk, oil and eggs. (Lightly spoon flour into measuring cup; level off.) Add flour, baking powder and salt. Beat until smooth. Heat an 8-inch crêpe pan* or fry pan over medium heat. Grease lightly. Pour 2 tablespoons at a time into fry pan; tilt to make a 6-inch round crêpe. Brown one minute, turn and brown other side. When all crêpes are prepared, fill them by placing a ham slice, a cheese slice and two asparagus spears on each crêpe; roll up. Place single layer, seam side down, in 13x9-inch baking dish. Preheat oven to 350°F. In medium saucepan, fry mushrooms in butter. Stir in 3 tablespoons flour. Add water, bouillon and cream. Cook, stirring constantly, until thickened. Stir in cheese and chives. Spoon Sauce over crêpes. Bake 20 to 30 minutes until hot and bubbly.

6 servings (12 crêpes)

*A variety of crêpe pans are available; follow manufacturer's directions.

TIP: Crêpes may be made in advance. Stack between paper toweling in a covered container and store in the refrigerator or freezer.

Country Cookin'
Frosty Fruit Cooler
Broiled Ham and Fruit Kabobs
Make-Ahead Waffle Batter
OR
Waffles

The refreshing Fruit Cooler is reminiscent of the old-fashioned fruit shrub and mighty appealing to all ages. While the golden-glazed kabobs are broiling to a turn, the fragrance of waffles a cookin' makes this a real country-style, down-home type meal. Why not offer a variety of syrups with the waffles along with some honey and a dish of Grandmother's homemade preserves?

FROSTY FRUIT COOLER

  1½ cups apricot nectar, chilled
  1½ cups pineapple or orange juice, chilled
  2 cups ginger ale
  1 cup pineapple or orange sherbet

In punch bowl or large (2 quart) container, combine apricot nectar and pineapple juice. Just before serving, stir in ginger ale and scoops of sherbet until smooth. Serve immediately.

8 (¾ cup) servings

TIP: For individual servings, place a scoop of sherbet in each glass. Fill glasses ¾ full with equal amounts of chilled apricot nectar and chilled pineapple or orange juice. Add chilled ginger ale to fill glass.

BROILED HAM AND FRUIT KABOBS

½ cup orange marmalade
  or apricot preserves
¼ cup orange juice
1 tablespoon lemon juice
½ teaspoon ground
  ginger, if desired
1½ cups (8 oz.) cooked ham,
  cut into 1-inch cubes
2 medium bananas, cut
  into 1-inch slices
8-oz. can pineapple
  chunks, drained

Combine marmalade, orange juice, lemon juice and ginger to make basting sauce; mix well. Thread ham, bananas and pineapple on 4 large or 8 small skewers, beginning and ending with ham. Grill or broil kabobs 6 to 8 inches from heat for 15 to 20 minutes. Brush frequently with basting sauce until ham and fruit are heated.

4 servings

TIP: If desired, let ham, bananas and pineapple marinate 1 to 2 hours in basting sauce before cooking.

An ideal batter to have in the refrigerator for carefree weekend breakfasts or brunches. Tastes and smells like sourdough.

MAKE AHEAD WAFFLE BATTER

2¼ cups Pillsbury's Best
  All Purpose or
  Unbleached Flour
1 pkg. active dry yeast
2 tablespoons sugar
1 teaspoon salt
2 cups milk
¼ cup butter or oil
3 eggs

(Lightly spoon flour into measuring cup; level off.) In large bowl, combine flour, yeast, sugar and salt. In saucepan, heat milk and butter until very warm (120° to 130°F.). Add to flour mixture along with eggs. Beat with mixer or beater until smooth. Cover and store in refrigerator up to 4 days, adding 2 additional tablespoons sugar after second day of storage. Bake in preheated waffle iron, set at medium heat, 5 to 8 minutes until steaming stops and waffle is golden brown.

4 waffles

TIPS: Be sure to refrigerate batter in *large* container because yeast "works" as it is stored and volume of batter increases.

If desired, use up to ½ whole grain flour.

HIGH ALTITUDE: No change.

WAFFLES

2 eggs, separated
2 cups buttermilk or
  sour milk*
2 cups Pillsbury's Best
  All Purpose or
  Unbleached Flour**
2 teaspoons baking
  powder
1 teaspoon soda
1 teaspoon salt
½ cup butter or
  margarine, melted, or
  cooking oil

Place egg yolks in large bowl; whites in small bowl. To yolks add buttermilk; beat well. (Lightly spoon flour into measuring cup; level off.) Add flour, baking powder, soda and salt; beat until smooth. Stir in melted butter. Beat egg whites until soft peaks form. Fold into batter. Bake in preheated waffle iron, set at medium heat, 5 to 8 minutes until steaming stops and waffle is golden brown.

4 waffles

*To sour milk, use 2 tablespoons vinegar plus enough milk to make 2 cups.

**With self-rising flour, omit baking powder and reduce soda to ½ teaspoon.

TIPS: Refrigerate or freeze leftover waffles. Reheat or thaw in toaster.

Up to ½ whole grain flour may be used.

For APPLE WAFFLES, add 1 medium apple, shredded, and ½ teaspoon cinnamon.

For BLUEBERRY WAFFLES, add 1 cup fresh or frozen drained blueberries to batter.

HIGH ALTITUDE — Above 3500 Feet: Reduce baking powder to 1 teaspoon.

A piggy-bank special...but no one will know but you. This is a marvelous fall and winter menu when appetites are hearty and canned fruits must suffice. As colorful as autumn leaves, the amber cider, golden cheese sauce and rosy glow of the cranberry relish add up to scrumptious eating and lots of eye appeal. If desired, Canadian bacon or small breakfast steaks can be added for a more elaborate repast.

Harvest Time
Hot Sunny Cider
Quick Filled Pears
Welsh Rarebit

Orange and pineapple juice add sunshine to this cider.

HOT SUNNY CIDER
 1 quart apple cider
 1 cup orange juice
 1 cup pineapple juice
 1 teaspoon whole allspice
 1 teaspoon whole cloves
 2 two-inch cinnamon sticks

In saucepan, combine all ingredients. Simmer 10 to 15 minutes. Strain. Serve in mugs. If desired, garnish with a cinnamon stick or orange slice in each mug.

6 (1 cup) servings

TIP: For Hot Cider Bracer, add 2 tablespoons (1 oz.) brandy to each serving.

Welsh Rarebit

QUICK FILLED PEARS

12 pear halves (two 1-pound, 13-oz. cans), drained
12 tablespoons frozen or canned cranberry orange relish
Lettuce leaves

Spoon 1 tablespoon cranberry orange relish into hollow of each pear half. On individual salad plates, arrange 2 filled pear halves on lettuce leaves. Refrigerate 15 minutes or until serving time.

6 servings

Be sure to cook Rarebit over low heat so cheese will not become stringy.

WELSH RAREBIT

3 tablespoons butter or margarine
3 cups (2 lb.) cubed American cheese
12-oz. can (1½ cups) beer
3 eggs, slightly beaten
1½ teaspoons dry mustard
1 teaspoon Worcestershire sauce, 6 drops Tabasco sauce, if desired
6 slices toast

In medium saucepan over low heat, melt butter. Add cheese and beer. Cook, stirring constantly, over very low heat until cheese melts. In small mixing bowl, combine beaten egg, mustard, Worcestershire and Tabasco sauces. Add slowly to melted cheese, beating with a wire whisk or rotary beater. Continue cooking, stirring occasionally, about 10 minutes until thickened. Serve over toast points.

6 servings

TIP: For an interesting variation serve over toast points and thin tomato slices. Top with crumbled bacon.

Hearty Hunt Brunch

Grapefruit-Cider Mist
Baked Eggs in Toast Cups
OR
Cook and Hold
Scrambled Eggs
Canadian-Style Bacon Bake
Sherried Peaches
Caramel-Orange Coffee Cake

The effervescent Mist is the perfect "eye-opener" for this full-course hunt-type brunch. The inviting menu offers two types of eggs, and the cook and hold variety is an answer to the hostess' prayer if serving time is uncertain. If you are serving buffet, put your appliances to good use; hot plates, chafing dishes, bunwarmers and coffee makers will keep your foods at the proper serving temperature and readily accessible to hungry guests.

GRAPEFRUIT CIDER MIST

3 cups grapefruit juice
1 cup apple cider
2½ cups gingerale
Lime slices and maraschino cherries, to garnish

Combine grapefruit juice and cider. Just before serving, add gingerale. Serve over ice cubes. Garnish with lime slices and maraschino cherries.

6 (1 cup) servings

Eggs bake quickly with little watching.

BAKED EGGS IN TOAST CUPS

6 slices white bread
6 eggs
6 tablespoons cream
Salt
Pepper
¾ cup (3 oz.) shredded Swiss cheese

Preheat oven to 350° F. Butter six individual baking dishes or custard cups. Remove crusts from bread; butter on both sides. Fit a slice of bread into each dish. Break one egg into each; spoon 1 tablespoon cream over each egg. Sprinkle with salt and pepper. Bake uncovered 15 to 20 minutes or until eggs are set. Sprinkle 2 tablespoons shredded cheese over each egg and return to oven just until cheese melts.

6 servings

No waste when using Canadian bacon, which helps justify the cost.

CANADIAN-STYLE BACON BAKE

1 to 1½ pounds Canadian bacon, unsliced
¼ cup firmly packed brown sugar
2 teaspoons flour
⅛ teaspoon dry mustard
1 teaspoon water

Place bacon in shallow baking pan. Bake uncovered at 350° F. for 20 minutes. Combine remaining ingredients; spread over bacon. Bake 20 minutes longer. Cut into thin slices.

6 to 8 servings

These eggs hold well for latecomers.
Remember to keep them covered.

COOK AND HOLD SCRAMBLED EGGS

¼ cup butter or margarine
12 eggs
1⅓ cups milk
1 teaspoon salt
⅛ teaspoon pepper
2 tablespoons flour
2 tablespoons chopped pimento
1 teaspoon chopped chives

In large fry pan, melt butter, tilting to coat pan. In blender, combine remaining ingredients. Mix until blended. Pour into fry pan. Cook over low heat, occasionally stirring from outside edge of pan to center to allow uncooked egg to flow to bottom of pan. Cook until set but still moist. To hold up to 2 hours, place in covered chafing dish over hot water, electric fry pan set at 200° F., or in covered casserole in 200° F. oven.

6 to 8 servings

TIP: Rotary beater may be used for combining ingredients.

A tart-sweet ginger and sherry
marinade turns a can of peaches into
something special.

SHERRIED PEACHES

6 peach halves (1-pound, 13-oz. can) drained, reserving ½ cup syrup
½ cup firmly packed brown sugar
¼ cup sugar
¼ teaspoon ground ginger
¼ teaspoon cinnamon
½ cup dry sherry
2 tablespoons lemon juice

In small saucepan, combine ½ cup peach syrup with remaining ingredients. Cook until sugar is dissolved. Pour over peach halves. Cover. Chill overnight or several days. To serve, remove peaches from sherry mixture. Save liquid for use another time.

6 servings

CARAMEL-ORANGE COFFEE CAKE

1 pkg. Pillsbury Hot Roll Mix
⅔ cup very warm milk (105°-115° F.)
2 teaspoons grated orange peel
2 eggs

Glaze

½ cup firmly packed brown sugar
¼ cup butter or margarine, softened
3 tablespoons chopped nuts
1 tablespoon grated orange peel
2 tablespoons corn syrup

Filling

⅓ cup firmly packed brown sugar
1 teaspoon cinnamon
2 tablespoons grated orange peel
2 tablespoons butter or margarine, softened

In large bowl, dissolve yeast from hot roll mix in warm milk. Stir in 2 teaspoons orange peel and eggs. Add flour mixture; blend well. Cover; let rise in warm place until light and doubled in size, 30 to 45 minutes. Grease (not oil) 12-cup fluted tube pan (non-stick finish pan, too). In small bowl, combine Glaze ingredients; mix well. Spread in greased pan. In same bowl, combine first three Filling ingredients; set aside. On floured surface, roll or press dough to 16x12-inch rectangle. Spread with butter. Sprinkle Filling mixture over dough. Starting with longer side, roll up tightly; seal edges. Cut into 16 slices. Stand nine slices with cut side against outside edge of pan and seven slices around inside edge. Cover; let rise in warm place until light and doubled in size, 30 to 45 minutes. Preheat oven to 375° F. (350° F. for colored pan). Bake 20 to 30 minutes until deep golden brown. Let stand upright in pan 5 minutes; turn onto serving plate.

10-inch ring coffee cake

HIGH ALTITUDE — above 3500 Feet: Bake at 400° F. for 30 to 35 minutes.

Who said sausage and eggs were old hat? This unique menu takes the humdrum out of that standard combination with a surprise bouquet of exotic flavors. The savory Sausage Wraps may be served with the drinks to satisfy hunger pangs while the omelet is being readied, or they may be passed at the table. These recipes are unusual and the proof is, of course, in the eating. So don't hesitate to give them a try (and have plenty for seconds in the kitchen)!

Garnish this "waker-upper" with lime slices and/or a thin stalk of celery.

BLOODY MARY

    1 quart tomato juice
    ⅔ cup (5 oz.) vodka
    1 tablespoon Worcestershire
       sauce
       Tabasco sauce
       Salt
       Pepper
    6 lime wedges

Combine first three ingredients in a pitcher with ice. Add Tabasco sauce, salt and pepper to taste. Serve over ice in glasses. Squeeze lime wedge and place in each glass.

6 (¾ cup) servings

Oriental Accent
Bloody Mary
Parmesan Sausage Wraps
Baked Omelet Oriental
Filled Melon Wedges

PARMESAN SAUSAGE WRAPS

    8-oz. can Pillsbury
       Refrigerated Quick Crescent
       Dinner Rolls
    ⅓ cup grated Parmesan cheese
    16 cocktail or Vienna sausages
    ¼ cup milk
       Sesame seed

Preheat oven to 375° F. Separate crescent dough into 8 triangles. Cut each in half lengthwise to make 16 triangles. Sprinkle each with 1 teaspoon Parmesan cheese. Place one cocktail sausage on wide end of each triangle and roll up. Dip in milk; place on greased cookie sheet. Sprinkle with sesame seed. Bake 10 to 12 minutes until golden brown. Serve hot.

16 snacks

TIP: To reheat, wrap in foil; heat at 375° F. for 5 to 10 minutes.

HIGH ALTITUDE: No change.

BAKED OMELET ORIENTAL

    Shrimp Filling (See below)
    Mustard Sauce (See below)
    6 eggs, separated
    ¼ teaspoon salt
    3 tablespoons water
    2 tablespoons butter or
       margarine

Prepare Filling and Sauce before preparing omelet. In mixing bowl, beat egg whites until stiff peaks form. In small bowl, beat egg yolks, salt and water. Fold into beaten whites. Preheat oven to 350° F. Heat butter in 10-inch ovenproof fry pan until sizzling, tilting to coat pan. Add egg mixture; spread over entire pan. Cook over medium heat until bottom is lightly browned. Bake, uncovered, 10 minutes or until top is dry and puffy. Loosen edge; mark fold. Spoon Filling over half of omelet; fold over. Lift gently out of pan. Serve immediately with Mustard Sauce.

4 servings

HIGH ALTITUDE: No change.

Shrimp Filling

    2 tablespoons chopped onion
    1 tablespoon chopped green
       pepper
    1 tablespoon butter or
       margarine
    ½ cup drained bean sprouts
    4½-oz. can (1 cup) tiny shrimp,
       drained
    ¼ teaspoon ground ginger
    1 tablespoon soy sauce

In small fry pan, fry onion and green pepper in butter until tender. Add remaining ingredients. Heat through. Cover and keep warm until omelet is baked.

1½ cups

Mustard Sauce

 2 tablespoons butter or margarine
 2 tablespoons flour
 4 teaspoons sugar
 2 teaspoons dry mustard
 ½ teaspoon salt
 1 cup milk
 1 tablespoon vinegar
 1 tablespoon snipped parsley
 2 to 3 drops yellow food coloring, if desired

In small saucepan, melt butter. Combine flour, sugar, mustard, salt and milk. Stir into butter and cook, stirring constantly, until thickened. Boil 1 minute. Stir in vinegar, parsley and food coloring. Cover and keep warm while omelet bakes.

1 cup

Select a firm, ripe melon for peak flavor and color. Or you may want to purchase it a few days ahead and allow it to ripen at room temperature.

FILLED MELON WEDGES

 3-oz. pkg. raspberry or strawberry-flavored gelatin
 2 cups pineapple juice
 1 ripe cantaloupe

Dissolve gelatin in 1 cup boiling pineapple juice. Add remaining juice. Cut cantaloupe in half; remove seeds. Remove fruit, leaving ½-inch shell. Chop fruit and stir into gelatin. Place cantaloupe shells in bowls to hold them steady when filled with gelatin. Fill shells with gelatin mixture. Chill until firm or overnight. Cut into slices or wedges to serve.

4 to 6 servings

Filled Melon Wedge

Bloody Mary
Baked Omelet Oriental, p. 13
Parmesan Sausage Wraps

Luncheon Ideas

"What's for lunch?" becomes more than a casual question when guests are coming and you want to show off a bit. A festive mid-day gathering need not be elaborate or expensive in order to strike just the right note. The luncheons we have suggested here are for every pocketbook and every occasion. Many of the recipes are completely or partially make-ahead, so you aren't knee-deep in last minute details when it's high noon and guests are due. And, most of the menus would be just as delightful for Sunday night suppers or other occasions when a lighter touch is in order.

For your "salad days," comes this beautiful French luncheon or supper treat, enhanced with subtle herbs in a vinaigrette dressing. It is a picturesque meal on a platter — colorful, nutritious and just hearty enough to satisfy noontime appetites. To accompany the salad, we have selected an all-time Bake-Off® favorite, Dilly Casserole Bread. After one delicious bite, you will know why it has remained so popular over the years. Although it is a yeast bread, you will find it easy to prepare and well worth the effort. The luscious dessert speaks for itself. Light and tart, it blends harmoniously with almost any entrée.

French 'n Fancy
Salad Nicoise
Dilly Casserole Bread
Orange-Filled
Angel Food Dessert

SALAD NICOISE
Vinaigrette Dressing
- ¾ cup salad oil
- ¾ cup tarragon white wine vinegar
- ¼ cup chopped green onion
- 2 tablespoons snipped fresh parsley
- 2 teaspoons salt
- 1 teaspoon dry mustard
- 1 teaspoon sugar
- ½ teaspoon tarragon, crushed
- 1 glove garlic, crushed

Salad
- 16-oz. can cut green beans, drained
- 2 quarts torn, mixed salad greens
- 2 tomatoes, sliced
- 2 to 3 hard-cooked eggs, cut into wedges
- 6½-oz. can white tuna, drained
- 3 to 4 anchovy fillets, drained
- 3 to 4 slices salami or summer sausage, cut into strips
- ½ cup ripe olives
- 1 cup tiny whole pickled beets, drained

Combine first 9 ingredients in container with tight cover. Shake well. Pour ½ cup over beans. Marinate 1 hour, chilling thoroughly. Toss salad greens with enough dressing to coat; place on two large platters. Drain marinated beans; arrange on salad greens with remaining ingredients.

6 to 8 servings

TIP: Select a combination of 3 salad greens from: head lettuce, romaine, leaf lettuce, curly endive or spinach.

Capers, artichoke hearts, green pepper strips or strips of boiled ham are also good in this salad.

Salad Nicoise
Dilly Casserole Bread

DILLY CASSEROLE BREAD

2½ to 3 cups Pillsbury's Best All Purpose or Unbleached Flour
2 tablespoons sugar
2 to 3 teaspoons instant minced onion
2 teaspoons dill seed
1¼ teaspoons salt
¼ teaspoon soda
1 pkg. active dry yeast
1 cup (8 oz.) cream style cottage cheese
¼ cup water
1 tablespoon butter or margarine
1 egg
Butter, softened
Coarse salt, if desired

In large bowl, combine 1 cup flour, sugar, onion, dill seed, salt, soda and dry yeast. In saucepan, heat cottage cheese, water and 1 tablespoon butter until very warm (120° to 130°F.). Add warm liquid and egg to flour mixture. Blend at low speed until moistened; beat 3 minutes at medium speed. By hand, stir in remaining 1½ to 2 cups flour to form a stiff batter. Cover; let rise in warm place until light and doubled in size, 45 to 65 minutes. Stir down dough. Turn into well-greased (not oiled) 1½ or 2-quart casserole. Cover; let rise in warm place until light and doubled in size, 30 to 45 minutes. Preheat oven to 350°F. Bake 35 to 40 minutes until golden brown. Remove from casserole. Brush warm loaf with butter or margarine and sprinkle with coarse salt.

1 round loaf

HIGH ALTITUDE — above 3500 Feet: Bake at 375°F. for 35 to 40 minutes.

ORANGE-FILLED ANGEL FOOD DESSERT

1 pkg. Pillsbury Angel Food Cake Mix
1 cup sugar
3 tablespoons cornstarch
¼ teaspoon salt
1½ cups water
½ cup orange juice
2 tablespoons lemon juice
1 egg, slightly beaten
1 tablespoon butter or margarine
1 tablespoon grated orange peel
1 teaspoon grated lemon peel
½ cup whipping cream, whipped
1 cup cut-up orange sections

Preheat oven to 325°F. Prepare angel food cake mix as directed on package, except divide between 2 ungreased 9x5-inch loaf pans. Bake 35 to 45 minutes. Invert immediately to cool. In saucepan, combine sugar, cornstarch and salt. Add water, orange juice, lemon juice and egg; mix well. Cook over medium heat, stirring constantly, until very thick. Boil 1 minute. Add butter, orange peel and lemon peel. Cool. Remove 1 loaf cake from pan and cut into 10 slices. Fold whipped cream and orange sections into cooked mixture. Line bottom of 9-inch square pan or serving dish with half of cake slices; top with half of filling. Cover with remaining cake slices, then remaining filling. Chill several hours or overnight. To serve, cut into squares. If desired, garnish with additional whipped cream and orange slices.

9 servings

TIP: Second angel food loaf cake may be frozen for later use. Leave cake in pan or place in rigid container to avoid crushing. Wrap and freeze.

A golden crust covers a crunchy and creamy oriental-style filling in this Bake-Off® luncheon favorite, Turkey-Crescent Amandine. You'll love the way it disguises leftover chicken or turkey for a special post-holiday treat. And, no need for rolls because the Crescent crust fills the bill. A festive, tart salad and the unique vegetable idea round out this people-pleasing plateful.

TURKEY AND CRESCENT AMANDINE

  3 cups cooked, cubed turkey or chicken
10 ¾-oz. can condensed cream of chicken or mushroom soup
  8-oz. can (1 cup) water chestnuts, drained and sliced, if desired
  4-oz. can (½ cup) mushroom stems and pieces, drained
  ⅔ cup mayonnaise or salad dressing
  ½ cup chopped celery
  ½ cup chopped onion or 2 tablespoons instant minced onion

Turkey Treat
Turkey-Crescent Amandine
Molded Cranapple Salad
Broccoli with
Poppy Seed Topping
Chocolate Mousse

  ½ cup dairy sour cream
  8-oz. can Pillsbury Refrigerated Quick Crescent Dinner Rolls
  ⅔ cup (3 oz.) shredded natural Swiss or American pasteurized process cheese
  ½ cup slivered or sliced almonds
  2 to 4 tablespoons butter or margarine, melted

In large saucepan, combine first 8 ingredients. Cook over medium heat until mixture is hot and bubbly; pour into ungreased 12x8-inch or 13x9-inch baking dish. Preheat oven to 375°F. Separate crescent dough into 2 rectangles. Place rectangles over hot chicken mixture. Combine remaining ingredients; spread over dough. Bake 20 to 25 minutes until crust is deep golden brown. Serve immediately.

6 servings

TIP: To reheat, cover loosely with foil; heat at 375°F. 20 to 25 minutes.

HIGH ALTITUDE: No change.

This salad would also be marvelous with your Thanksgiving or Christmas turkey or with a succulent pork roast.

MOLDED CRANAPPLE SALAD

  6-oz. pkg. cherry or raspberry-flavored gelatin
  1 cup boiling water
  1 cup cranberry juice
  ½ teaspoon salt
10-oz. pkg. (1¼ cups) frozen cranberry-orange relish
  2 cups (2 medium) chopped apple

Dissolve gelatin in boiling water. Stir in remaining ingredients. Chill until mixture thickens; stir again. Pour into 4-cup mold. Chill until firm, 4 hours or overnight.

6 to 8 servings

BROCCOLI WITH POPPY SEED TOPPING

    2 tablespoons chopped
        onion
    2 tablespoons butter or
        margarine
    2 pkgs. (10 oz. each)
        frozen broccoli spears
    1 cup dairy sour cream
    2 teaspoons sugar
    ½ to 1 teaspoon poppy seed
    ¼ teaspoon salt
        Toasted almonds, if
        desired

In saucepan, cook onion in butter until golden. Add broccoli; cover and simmer 8 to 10 minutes until tender. Remove broccoli to serving dish; season to taste. In same saucepan, add sour cream, sugar, poppy seed and salt. Stir over low heat until warm; do not boil. Spoon over broccoli. Sprinkle with toasted almonds, if desired.

6 to 8 servings

If desired, substitute 2 tablespoons brandy, white créme de menthe, créme de cacao or Cognac for vanilla.

CHOCOLATE MOUSSE

    1 cup milk
    1 envelope
        (1 tablespoon) unflavored
        gelatin
    2 squares semi-sweet
        chocolate or ⅓ cup semi-
        sweet chocolate pieces
    ⅓ cup sugar
    3 eggs, separated
    ⅛ teaspoon salt
    1 teaspoon vanilla
    ⅓ cup sugar
    1 cup whipping cream

Combine milk and gelatin; let stand while melting chocolate in saucepan over low heat. Stir ⅓ cup sugar and milk mixture into chocolate. Beat in egg yolks and salt. Cook over medium heat, stirring constantly, until mixture thickens slightly and coats a metal spoon. Add vanilla and cool. In mixing bowl, beat egg whites until frothy. Gradually beat in ⅓ cup sugar until mixture forms stiff peaks. Fold egg whites into cooled chocolate mixture. In large bowl, beat cream until thickened. Fold chocolate mixture into whipped cream. Spoon into 6 to 8 individual serving dishes or 1 large serving dish. Chill 2 to 3 hours before serving.

6 to 8 servings

Busy Day Delight

Easy Chicken and Matzo Balls
Spicy Peach Salad
Confetti Cheese Bread
Tapioca Pudding

Long a delicious tradition in many homes, the chicken and matzo ball recipe is simmered to tenderness in a time-saving pressure cooker. Pumpkin pie spice is the secret ingredient in the peachy salad, and the savory bread is a busy-day bonanza with Pillsbury biscuits forming the super-easy loaf. Tapioca can be as plain or as fancy as you wish — just look at all the variations!

EASY CHICKEN AND MATZO BALLS

    2½ to 3 pounds chicken, cut
        into pieces
    4 cups water
    1 tablespoon salt
    1 onion, sliced
    1 stalk celery, cut into
        pieces
    4½-oz. pkg. matzo ball and
        soup mix

In pressure cooker, combine chicken, water, salt, onion, celery and soup packet from mix. Cook as directed in pressure cooker manual for medium doneness. Meanwhile, prepare matzo ball mix as directed on package. Form into 1½ to 2-inch balls. Place on hot liquid; cover. Simmer as directed on package (without lifting cover) until balls are cooked through. Serve broth in bowls with chicken pieces and matzo balls.

4 to 5 servings

SPICY PEACH SALAD

   3-oz. pkg. orange-flavored gelatin
   ¼ teaspoon pumpkin pie spice or cinnamon
   1 cup boiling water
   10-oz. pkg. (1⅓ cups) frozen peach slices, unthawed
   Lettuce

In medium bowl, combine dry gelatin and pumpkin pie spice. Add boiling water; stir until dissolved. Add frozen peach slices; stir until peaches are thawed. Pour into 1-quart mold or 8-inch square pan. Chill until firm. Serve on lettuce leaves.

4 servings

CONFETTI CHEESE BREAD

   2 tablespoons butter or margarine
   ⅓ cup shredded Cheddar cheese
   ¼ cup chopped green pepper
   2 tablespoons imitation bacon bits, if desired
   2 tablespoons chopped pimento
   1 teaspoon instant minced onion
   8-oz. can Pillsbury Refrigerated Buttermilk or Country Style Biscuits

Preheat oven to 400°F. In medium size saucepan, melt butter. Add cheese, pepper, bacon bits, pimento and onion. Separate dough into 10 biscuits; cut each biscuit into 4 pieces. Drop a few biscuit quarters at a time unto cheese mixture while tossing lightly with forks. Turn into well-greased 8-inch round pan; distribute evenly. Bake 18 to 20 minutes until golden brown. Cool 5 minutes before removing from pan. Serve warm or cold.

1 round loaf

HIGH ALTITUDE: No change.

TAPIOCA PUDDING

   2 eggs, separated
   2 cups milk
   ¼ cup sugar
   3 tablespoons quick-cooking tapioca
   ¼ teaspoon salt
   1 teaspoon vanilla
   2 tablespoons sugar

In saucepan, combine egg yolks, milk, ¼ cup sugar, tapioca and salt; mix well. Cook over medium heat until mixture comes to a full boil, stirring constantly. Remove from heat. Blend in vanilla. In bowl, beat egg whites until frothy. Gradually add 2 tablespoons sugar; beat until mixture forms soft peaks. Fold into tapioca mixture just until well-combined. Spoon into serving dishes. Cool.

4 to 5 servings.

TIP: If desired, fold in ½ cup finely chopped dates, peaches, apricots, strawberries, raspberries or other fruit.

A pot of soup simmering on the stove and a Hero Sandwich in the making — a he-man luncheon for big appetites and cool weather. The sandwich goes well with either soup, so take your choice and try the other recipe on another occasion. Begin soup preparation well in advance of serving so meat and vegetables are tender and flavors well-blended. The delicious, fruity bars need no frosting — just a light dusting of powdered sugar. You will want to repeat all these recipes for casual supper entertaining, too! Great for after skiing.

OLD-FASHIONED VEGETABLE SOUP

2 to 3 pounds beef shank or meaty soup bones
3 teaspoons salt
¼ teaspoon leaf thyme or marjoram
6 peppercorns or ¼ teaspoon pepper
2 whole allspice
1 bay leaf
2 cubes or 2 teaspoons beef bouillon
2 quarts (8 cups) water
2 medium potatoes, peeled and cubed
2 stalks celery, sliced
2 medium carrots, sliced
1 small onion, chopped
16-oz. can (2 cups) tomatoes, undrained
12-oz. can (1½ cups) whole kernel corn, drained, if desired

"Souper" Sampler
Old-Fashioned Vegetable Soup
OR
Ham and Split Pea Soup
Hero Sandwich
Apricot-Banana Bars

In large saucepan, combine first 8 ingredients. Cover and simmer 2½ to 3 hours or until meat is tender. Remove beef shank, peppercorns, allspice and bay leaf. Cut meat from bones and return to soup. Add remaining ingredients; cover and simmer 30 minutes or until vegetables are tender.

6 to 8 (1½-cup) servings

HAM AND SPLIT PEA SOUP

16-oz. pkg. (2 cups) split peas
2 pounds ham shank
½ teaspoon salt
½ teaspoon leaf basil
¼ teaspoon pepper
2 quarts (8 cups) water
2 medium stalks celery, sliced
1 small onion, chopped
1 medium carrot, finely chopped, if desired

In large saucepan, combine all ingredients. Cover and simmer 1½ to 2 hours or until peas are tender and soup thickens. Remove ham shank, cut meat from bone and return to soup.

6 to 8 (1½-cup) servings

A mouth-watering combo of ingredients that tastes terrific hot or cold.

HERO SANDWICH

14-inch loaf French or Italian bread
8-oz. pkg. braunschweiger
4 to 6 slices Swiss cheese
4 to 6 thin slices cooked ham
1 large Bermuda onion, thinly sliced
1 large tomato, thinly sliced
4 to 6 lettuce leaves
4 hard-cooked eggs, chopped
¼ cup mayonnaise or salad dressing
¼ cup chopped sweet pickle
¼ cup chopped celery
½ teaspoon salt
Dash pepper

Cut bread in half lengthwise. Spread braunschweiger evenly over bottom half of loaf. Arrange slices of cheese, ham, onion, tomato and lettuce over braunschweiger. Combine eggs, mayonnaise, pickle, celery, salt and pepper. Spread over lettuce. Replace top half of bread. Cut diagonally into 6 to 8 portions.

6 to 8 servings

TIP: Vary filling by substituting sliced salami, bologna, meat loaf, turkey or other cold cuts and/or sliced green pepper rings.

For HOT HERO SANDWICH, use turkey, ham, cheese and onion for filling. Wrap in foil. Bake at 350°F. 20 to 25 minutes.

Old-Fashioned Vegetable Soup

APRICOT-BANANA BARS

½ cup butter or margarine, softened
1 cup firmly packed brown sugar
¾ cup apricot preserves
2 eggs
1 teaspoon vanilla
1¾ cups Pillsbury's Best All Purpose or Unbleached Flour
1 teaspoon baking powder
½ teaspoon soda
¼ teaspoon salt
¾ cup mashed ripe banana
½ cup chopped nuts
Powdered sugar

Preheat oven to 350°F. Grease (not oil) and flour 15x10-inch jelly roll pan. In mixing bowl, blend butter and brown sugar. Beat in preserves, eggs and vanilla. (Lightly spoon flour into measuring cup; level off.) Stir in remaining ingredients. Spread in prepared pan. Bake 25 to 30 minutes or until toothpick inserted in center comes out clean. Cool. Sprinkle with powdered sugar.

3 dozen bars

TIP: Sprinkle powdered sugar through a small strainer to give it an even appearance.

HIGH ALTITUDE — above 3500 Feet: Reduce baking powder to ¾ teaspoon. Bake at 350°F. 25 to 30 minutes.

European Encore

Gazpacho
Quiche Lorraine
Pineapple Boats
Chocolate-Almond Butterballs
Cream Cheese-Jam Bars

Another special luncheon menu — this one tastefully accented with classical recipes from our European heritage. Contrasted with the bold color and piquant flavor of the soup, the Quiche offers a mild combination of Swiss cheese and bacon. And, no worry about turning out a perfect crust with Crescent Rolls forming the easy-do shell. A light, white wine would be a festive touch with the Quiche. The refreshing Pineapple Boats may be used for a salad or as dessert, served with two of our favorite sweet treats.

This "liquid salad" makes tasty use of fresh garden vegetables. It is nutritious, refreshing and low in calories, too!

GAZPACHO

3 cups (24-oz. can) tomato-vegetable juice
1 cucumber, thinly sliced
½ green pepper, chopped
2 medium tomatoes, chopped, if desired
1 small onion, chopped
1 tablespoon oil or olive oil
1 tablespoon wine vinegar or lemon juice
1 clove garlic, minced
Dash Tabasco sauce

Combine all ingredients and chill thoroughly, at least 6 hours. Serve chilled.

5 to 6 (¾-cup) servings

QUICHE LORRAINE

8-oz. can Pillsbury Refrigerated Quick Crescent Dinner Rolls
3½-oz. can French fried onions
1 egg, beaten
1 cup light cream or evaporated milk
½ teaspoon salt
½ teaspoon Worcestershire sauce
1 cup (4 oz.) shredded Swiss cheese
9 slices bacon, fried and crumbled

Preheat oven to 375°F. Separate crescent dough into 8 triangles. Place in ungreased 9-inch pie pan or quiche pan; press over bottom and up sides to form crust. Sprinkle with half of French fried onions. Combine egg, cream, salt and Worcestershire sauce. Stir in cheese. Pour egg mixture into crust. Sprinkle with bacon and remaining onions. Bake 25 to 30 minutes (40 to 45 minutes for quiche pan) or until knife inserted near center comes out clean. Cool 5 minutes before cutting into wedges to serve.

9-inch pie

TIP: One cup cubed, cooked ham, luncheon meat, shrimp or crab meat may be substituted for bacon. Garnish plate with carrot curls and parsley.

HIGH ALTITUDE: No change.

Fresh pineapple makes attractive holders for fruit salads or desserts.

PINEAPPLE BOATS
    1 fresh pineapple
    1 pint sherbet (lemon,
      lime or pineapple)

With sharp knife, cut pineapple into quarters lengthwise through stem. Remove fruit, using a grapefruit or serated knife; leave a ½-inch thick shell. Cut fruit into chunks, discarding "eyes" and core. Fill shells with balls of sherbet; top with pineapple chunks.

4 servings

TIP: Chill remaining pineapple chunks in covered container for later use.

CHOCOLATE-ALMOND BUTTERBALLS
    2 squares (1 oz. each)
      semi-sweet chocolate
    1 tablespoon milk
    ¾ cup butter or margarine,
      softened
    ½ cup sugar
    2 teaspoons vanilla
    2 cups Pillsbury's Best All
      Purpose or Unbleached
      Flour
    ¼ teaspoon salt
    ½ cup chopped almonds
      or nuts
      Sugar

Preheat oven to 350°F. Melt chocolate with milk over low heat; cool. In mixing bowl, cream butter, sugar and vanilla. Blend in cooled chocolate mixture. (Lightly spoon flour into measuring cup; level off.) Stir in flour, salt and almonds until well-mixed. Shape into balls, using a rounded teaspoonful of dough for each. Roll in sugar; place 2 inches apart on ungreased cookie sheets. Bake 12 to 15 minutes until firm.

4 to 5 dozen cookies

TIPS: If desired, substitute ⅓ cup semi-sweet chocolate pieces for squares of chocolate.

   Whole grain flour may be used, but reduce amount to 1¾ cups.

HIGH ALTITUDE — above 3500 Feet: Bake at 375°F. 12 to 15 minutes.

The choice of flavor is yours when you make these versatile bars. We especially like apricot filling.

CREAM CHEESE JAM BARS
    2 cups Pillsbury's Best All
      Purpose or Unbleached
      Flour
    1 cup sugar
    2 teaspoons baking
      powder
    ½ teaspoon salt
    ½ cup butter or margarine,
      softened
    1 egg

Filling
    8-oz. pkg. cream cheese,
      softened
    ½ cup strawberry, peach
      or apricot preserves

Preheat oven to 350°F. Grease (not oil) 13x9-inch pan. (Lightly spoon flour into measuring cup; level off.) In large bowl, combine first 6 ingredients; blend at low speed until crumbly. Press 2 cups crumb mixture into greased pan. In small bowl, blend Filling ingredients until smooth. Spread evenly over crust. Sprinkle with reserved crumb mixture; press lightly. Bake 25 to 30 minutes until golden brown. Cool; cut into bars. Store in refrigerator.

2 to 3 dozen bars

HIGH ALTITUDE — above 3500 Feet: Bake at 375°F. 25 to 35 minutes.

You'll have all the guests vying for your recipes when you serve this spectacular menu — so perfect when you are honoring the bride-to-be or hostessing any other "ladies only" celebration. With almost all the preparation completed before guests arrive, you will be free to pour your friends a sherry or tomato juice "starter" while things are heating. They will appreciate your attention and will be very impressed with your cool efficiency.

Garnish this colorful treat with lemon wedges and sprigs of parsley.

CRAB ROYALE

2 cups (16 oz.) cooked crabmeat, drained and flaked
1 cup (4 oz.) shredded Cheddar or Swiss cheese
⅓ cup dry bread crumbs
½ cup chopped celery
½ cup salad dressing or mayonnaise
⅓ cup milk or light cream
3 tablespoons chopped pimento, if desired
3 tablespoons chopped green pepper, if desired
1½ teaspoons instant minced onion
1½ teaspoons lemon juice
¼ teaspoon salt
Dash pepper

Preheat oven to 375°F. In medium mixing bowl, combine all ingredients; mix well. Spoon into 6

Seafood Spectacular
Crab Royale
Asparagus Vinaigrette
Butterflake Herb Rolls
Angel Pie

shells or small baking dishes. Bake 12 to 15 minutes until lightly browned and heated through.

6 servings

TIP: To make ahead, prepare, cover and refrigerate. Bake 20 minutes.

ASPARAGUS VINAIGRETTE

⅓ cup bottled oil and vinegar salad dressing
1 tablespoon finely chopped green pepper
1 tablespoon sweet pickle relish
1 teaspoon finely chopped onion
2 cans (15 oz. each) extra-long green asparagus spears, chilled and drained
12 to 16 cherry tomatoes
½ ripe avocado, sliced and dipped in lemon juice
6 to 8 marinated artichoke hearts
Lettuce

Combine first 4 ingredients. Arrange asparagus, tomatoes, avocado slices and artichoke hearts on individual lettuce-lined salad plates. Drizzle with dressing mixture.

6 servings

BUTTERFLAKE HERB ROLLS

8-oz can Pillsbury Refrigerated Quick Butterflake Dinner Rolls
1 tablespoon butter or margarine, melted
1 tablespoon snipped parsley or 1½ teaspoons parsley flakes
½ teaspoon caraway or poppy seed

Preheat oven to 375°F. Place rolls in 6 greased (not oiled) muffin pans as directed on label. Brush with melted butter; sprinkle with parsley and caraway seed. Bake 12 to 14 minutes until golden brown. Serve warm.

6 rolls

HIGH ALTITUDE: No change.

Make ahead and chill overnight to let the crust soften and mellow for ease in serving. Elegant!

ANGEL PIE

- 3 eggs, separated
- ⅛ teaspoon cream of tartar
- ¾ cup sugar

Filling

- ½ cup sugar
- 1 tablespoon grated lemon peel
- 3 tablespoons lemon juice
- 3 reserved egg yolks
- 1 cup whipping cream, whipped

Grease (not oil) 9-inch pie pan. In small bowl, beat egg whites (reserve yolks) with cream of tartar until frothy. Gradually add ¾ cup sugar, beating until stiff peaks form. Spread over bottom and sides of greased pie pan. Meringue puffs up during baking, so spread only to top edge of pan. Bake at 275°F. for 60 minutes. Turn oven off. Leave crust in oven to cool and dry. In saucepan, combine Filling ingredients except whipped cream.

Cook over low heat, stirring constantly until thickened. Cool. Fold into whipped cream. Pour into meringue shell. Refrigerate overnight. If desired, garnish with thin lemon slices or grated lemon peel.

9-inch pie

TIP: Two cups (4½-oz. pkg.) frozen whipped topping may be substituted for whipped cream.

HIGH ALTITUDE: No change.

Angel Pie

Another featured recipe where no one would guess you were using leftover poultry in this creamy, delicious Italian casserole. The Tetrazzini is easy on the budget and adapts beautifully to buffet serving. A choice make-ahead salad, terrific any time of year, and Pillsbury's quick-as-a-wink Braided Bread Stick recipe add color and crunchy contrast to this very inviting luncheon menu. Chocolate lovers will applaud the rich, dark dessert which holds a surprise cream cheese ribbon to make it extra moist and attractive.

Note TIP on day-ahead preparation to give you more free time the morning of your luncheon.

CHICKEN TETRAZZINI
   7 to 8-oz pkg. spaghetti
   2 cups (16 oz.) sliced fresh mushrooms or 1 cup canned mushrooms
   4 tablespoons butter or margarine
   2 tablespoons flour
   2 cups chicken broth
   1 cup light cream or evaporated milk
   3 tablespoons sherry, if desired
   1 teaspoon salt
   ⅛ teaspoon nutmeg
   Dash pepper
   3 cups cooked cubed chicken or turkey
   ¼ cup grated Parmesan cheese

Cook spaghetti as directed on package; drain. In fry pan, cook mushrooms in 2 tablespoons butter

For the Ladies
Chicken Tetrazzini
Orange Sherbet Salad
Braided Bread Sticks
Fudge Ribbon Cake

until tender. Add to spaghetti. In same pan, melt remaining 2 tablespoons butter; blend in flour. Stir in chicken broth. Cook, stirring constantly until sauce thickens; boil 1 minute. Remove from heat; stir in cream, sherry and seasonings. Pour half of sauce into spaghetti and mushrooms. Stir chicken into remaining sauce. Turn spaghetti mixture into greased 12x8-inch baking dish or shallow 2-quart casserole. Make a well in the center. Pour chicken mixture into well. Sprinkle with cheese. Bake at 375°F, uncovered, 30 minutes or until heated through.

6 to 8 servings

TIP: May be prepared, covered and refrigerated 1 day ahead. Bake, uncovered, 40 minutes.

You will be pleased with the refreshing, tart taste sensation.

ORANGE SHERBET SALAD
   6-oz. pkg. orange-flavored gelatin
   ¾ cup boiling water
   ¾ cup orange juice
   2 cups (1 pint) orange sherbet
   11-oz. can (1 cup) mandarin oranges, drained
   Lettuce

In small bowl, dissolve gelatin in boiling water. Add orange juice and sherbet, blend at low speed until mixture is smooth. Stir in oranges. Chill until thickened but not set. Stir again. Pour into 8-inch square pan. Chill until firm, about 4 hours or overnight. To serve, cut into squares and place on lettuce-lined salad plates.

6 to 8 servings

They won't believe you made your own breadsticks. Note the exciting variations under TIPS.

BRAIDED BREAD STICKS
   8-oz. can Pillsbury Refrigerated Buttermilk or Country Style Biscuits
   2 tablespoons butter or margarine, melted
   Coarse salt

Preheat oven to 400°F. Separate biscuit dough into 10 biscuits. Cut each biscuit into thirds. Roll each third into a 6-inch strip. Braid 3 strips together, pinching ends together. Place on ungreased cookie sheet. Brush with butter; sprinkle with salt. Bake 12 to 15 minutes until golden brown.

20 bread sticks

TIP: Substitute caraway seed, sesame seed, Parmesan cheese or poppy seed for coarse salt.
HIGH ALTITUDE: No change.

FUDGE RIBBON CAKE

8-oz. pkg. cream cheese, softened
¼ cup sugar
1 tablespoon cornstarch
2 tablespoons milk
½ teaspoon vanilla
1 egg

Cake

2 cups Pillsbury's Best All Purpose or Unbleached Flour
2 cups sugar
1 teaspoon salt
1 teaspoon baking powder
½ teaspoon soda
1⅓ cups milk
½ cup butter or margarine, softened
1 teaspoon vanilla

4 envelopes premelted chocolate or 4 squares unsweetened chocolate, melted
2 eggs

Frosting

¼ cup butter or margarine
¼ cup milk
1 teaspon vanilla
6-oz. pkg. (1 cup) semi-sweet chocolate pieces
2 cups powdered sugar

Preheat oven to 350°F. Grease (not oil) and flour bottom of 13x9-inch pan. In small bowl, combine first 6 ingredients. Beat 2 minutes at medium speed until smooth and creamy; set aside. (Lightly spoon flour into measuring cup; level off.) In large bowl, combine Cake ingredients; beat 3 minutes at medium speed. Pour half of batter (about 2½ cups) into prepared pan. Spoon cream cheese mixture over batter; spread carefully to cover batter. Spoon remaining batter by teaspoonsful uniformly over cream cheese layer; spread as evenly as possible. Bake 50 to 60 minutes until toothpick inserted in center comes out clean. Cool. In small saucepan, heat butter and milk to boiling; remove from heat. Stir in vanilla and chocolate pieces until smooth. Blend in powdered sugar until smooth. If necessary, thin with milk to spreading consistency. Spread over cooled cake. Store in refrigerator.

13x9-inch cake

HIGH ALTITUDE: No change.

Fudge Ribbon Cake

Teas & Receptions

Afraid of formality? Don't be. As they say, "There is a time and a place for almost everything," and there are bound to be special occasions in your life when you want tradition at the fore and elegance in the lead. Nowadays, many a bride and groom opt for the intimacy of a lovely home or garden reception and often, anniversary celebrations are warmer and friendlier if guests are gathered in a home rather than a hall. Other occasions? Baptismal receptions, graduations, a welcome home or farewell party or a house warming — all can be easily planned with the white glove approach and few last minute details to harass the hostess. "Planning" and "organization" are the key words and the success secrets to a sparkling party. Start setting the stage days before the event by checking your "inventory." Is the glassware adequate and spotless? Are linens pressed and is the silver polished? Order flowers, if necessary, and do as much marketing and food preparation as possible in advance. Be definite about the time span for your party when you issue the invitations so your guests are not in doubt. For teas and afternoon receptions, suitable hours are 2 to 4 p.m. or 3 to 5 p.m. For cocktail parties, aim for 5 to 7 p.m. or somewhat later on weekdays to accommodate those coming from the office. Guests may arrive a little late for such gatherings but are expected to depart very close to the suggested time. Although these types of parties last a relatively short time — just part of an afternoon or evening — they are marvelous ways to open your home to large groups of friends and celebrate a special occasion at the same time.

ABOUT TEAS

Tea always has been the traditional beverage for receptions and formal occasions, and much fuss has been made in regard to the proper method of brewing. There are three rules to remember when preparing tea:

- Water should be cold and freshly drawn. Never let it stand in the pot while you go about other preparations.
- Heat the water just to boiling. To release the full tea flavor, the water must be boiling when it is poured on the leaves. However, water that boils too long or has been reheated becomes flat tasting.
- Steep the tea no less than 3 minutes and no longer than 5 minutes. Follow the clock rather than the color since different teas produce different colors.

TYPES OF TEA

There are many commercial varieties of teas which vary among the locality, age of tea, manufacture, blending and addition of spices and herbs. We have listed a few of the more popular varieties.

BLACK: The most popular tea in this country. Has a rich aroma and mild flavor. Through a special treatment, the leaves oxidize and turn black.

ORANGE PEKOE: Perhaps the most familiar example of black tea. Pekoe refers to the size of the tea leaf.

OOLONG: Has a delicate flavor and light color. The leaves are allowed to partially oxidize, making them a greenish-brown color.

GREEN: Gives a brew pale green in color with a pungent flavor. Green tea is not oxidized.

DARJEELING: An Indian Black tea.

EARL GREY BLEND: A tea from China with a hint of orange flavor.

ENGLISH BREAKFAST: A delicately-flavored black tea from China, also called Keemun.

FORMOSA OOLONG: Has a strong bouquet and flavor.

LAPSANG SOUCHONG: A Chinese tea with a heavy smoky flavor.

CHAMOMILE: A somewhat bitter tea, often sweetened with honey or sugar.

JASMINE: Fragrant blossoms are added to this pungent, scented brew.

ROSE-HIP: A strongly-flavored tea made from the dried fruit of the rose; a source of vitamin C.

BASIC TEA RECIPE (One serving)

Boiling water
1 teaspoon tea leaves or
1 tea bag
5-6 oz. water, cold

Preheat a clean pottery or heat-resistant serving pot by filling with boiling water; let stand to warm pot. Meanwhile, heat cold water just to boiling. (Do not use a copper, brass or iron pot.) Pour out water in serving pot, add tea leaves and cover with freshly-boiled water. Steep 3 to 5 minutes. Remove tea bags or strain tea leaves. Serve immediately. Do not reheat tea or reuse tea leaves or bags.

Recipe may be increased to the desired number of servings.

TEA FOR MANY GUESTS

(25 servings)
½ cup tea leaves or
20 tea bags
4½ qt. water, cold

Follow directions as for Basic Tea Recipe. Keep tea warm on lowest heat if not serving immediately. Do not reheat to boiling.

ICED TEA

Follow Basic Tea Recipe, steeping the full 5 minutes. Strain and pour over ice cubes. If a weaker tea is desired, add additional water.

TIP: When tea is steeped or cooled too long, it sometimes becomes cloudy when added to ice. Just add a small amount of boiling water to make it clear again.

BUTTERY LACE COOKIES

½ cup butter or margarine
¾ cup quick-cooking rolled oats
½ cup sugar
¼ cup flour
2 tablespoons milk

Preheat oven to 375° F. In saucepan, melt butter. Stir in remaining ingredients. Cook, stirring constantly, just until mixture begins to bubble. Drop by level teaspoonful into ungreased muffin cups. Bake 5 to 6 minutes until light golden brown. Cool 2 minutes; while still warm, remove from muffin cups.

3 dozen cookies

HIGH ALTITUDE: — above 3500 Feet: Bake at 400° F. 5 to 6 minutes. Cool 1 minute; remove from muffin cups.

These traditional cookies (also called Mexican Wedding Cakes and Russian Teacakes) are a deluxe treat for the tea table.

SWEDISH TEA CAKES

1 cup butter or margarine, softened
½ cup powdered sugar
2 teaspoons vanilla
2 cups Pillsbury's Best All Purpose or Unbleached Flour
¼ teaspoon salt
1 cup finely chopped or ground almonds or pecans

Preheat oven to 325° F. In bowl, cream butter, powdered sugar and vanilla. (Lightly spoon flour into measuring cup; level off.) Blend in flour, salt and nuts until dough holds together. Shape into 1-inch balls. Place 1 inch apart on ungreased cookie sheets. Bake 15 to 20 minutes until set but not brown.

Cool slightly; roll in powdered sugar. Cool completely; roll again in powdered sugar.

5 dozen cookies

HIGH ALTITUDE: No change.

One of the fastest, sweetest bars you've ever tried!

CHOCOLATE TOFFEE CRESCENT BARS

8-oz. can Pillsbury Refrigerated Quick Crescent Dinner Rolls
⅔ cup firmly packed brown sugar
⅔ cup butter or margarine
1 to 1½ cups nut halves or chopped nuts
6-oz. pkg. (1 cup) milk chocolate or semi-sweet chocolate pieces

Preheat oven to 375° F. Separate crescent dough into 2 rectangles. Place in ungreased 15x10-inch jelly roll pan. Gently press dough to cover bottom of pan; seal perforations. In small saucepan, combine brown sugar and butter; boil 1 minute. Pour evenly over dough. Sprinkle with nuts. Bake 14 to 18 minutes until golden brown. Remove from oven; immediately sprinkle with chocolate pieces. Slightly swirl pieces as they melt, leaving some pieces partially melted or whole. (Do not spread evenly; leave a mottled appearance.) Cool; cut into bars.

3 to 4 dozen bars

HIGH ALTITUDE: No change.

For lemon lovers everywhere.

LEMON TWIST BARS

    1 pkg. Pillsbury Rich 'n Easy Creamy Lemon Frosting Mix (reserve part for Filling)

    1½ cups Pillsbury's Best All Purpose or Unbleached Flour

    ¾ cup butter or margarine

Glaze

    3 eggs

    Remaining frosting mix

    ¼ cup flour*

    ½ teaspoon baking powder

    6-oz. can frozen lemonade concentrate, thawed

(This recipe performs satisfactorily only with Pillsbury frosting mix.) Preheat oven to 350° F. (325° F. for glass). (To measure frosting mix and flour, lightly spoon into measuring cup; level off.) In medium bowl, combine 1 cup frosting mix and 1½ cups flour. Cut in butter to form fine crumbs. Press crumb mixture into ungreased 13x9-inch pan. Bake 17 to 20 minutes until light golden brown. Cool slightly. In large bowl, beat eggs; blend in remaining ingredients until smooth. Pour over crust. Bake 20 to 25 minutes until thin crust forms on top. If desired, sprinkle with powdered sugar. Cool; cut into bars.

2 to 3 dozen bars

*If using Pillsbury's Best Self-Rising Flour, omit baking powder.

HIGH ALTITUDE — above 3500 Feet: Bake at 375° F. for 17 to 20 minutes and 20 to 25 minutes.

The filling in these bars is as creamy and tastes as great as a chocolate malt!

CHOCOLATE MALT BARS

    2 cups Pillsbury's Best All Purpose or Unbleached Flour*

    1 cup sugar

    ½ cup firmly packed brown sugar

    1 teaspoon baking powder

    ½ teaspoon salt

    ¾ cup butter or margarine

    1 egg

    ¾ cup chopped nuts, if desired

Filling

    1 pkg. Pillsbury Rich 'n Easy Creamy Milk Chocolate or Fudge Frosting Mix

    ⅓ cup instant malted milk mix

    8-oz. pkg. cream cheese, softened

    ¼ cup milk

    1 egg

Preheat oven to 350° F. (Lightly spoon flour into measuring cup; level off.) In large bowl, combine first seven ingredients; blend at low speed until crumbly. Stir in nuts. Reserve 1 cup crumb mixture; press remainder into ungreased 13x9-inch pan. In large bowl, combine Filling ingredients; beat until smooth. Pour over crumb crust. Sprinkle remaining crumb mixture over Filling. Bake 40 to 45 minutes until golden brown. Chill; cut into bars. Store in refrigerator.

2 to 3 dozen bars

*If using Pillsbury's Best Self-Rising Flour, omit baking powder and salt.

HIGH ALTITUDE: — above 3500 Feet: Reduce sugar to ¾ cup and butter or margarine to ½ cup. Bake at 350° F. 40 to 45 minutes.

GLAZED SALTED ALMONDS

    1 egg white, slightly beaten

    1 tablespoon butter or margarine, melted

    2 cups blanched almonds

    Salt

    Grated Parmesan cheese

Blend egg white and butter; stir in nuts. Spread in shallow baking pan; sprinkle with salt and Parmesan cheese. Bake at 375° F. for 15 to 20 minutes until heated and glazed; watch closely and stir often to prevent burning.

2 cups

APRICOT JEWELS

    ½ cup butter or margarine, softened

    3-oz. pkg. cream cheese, softened

    ¼ cup sugar

    1¼ cups Pillsbury's Best All Purpose or Unbleached Flour

    1½ teaspoons baking powder

    ¼ teaspoon salt

    ½ cup apricot preserves

    ½ cup flaked coconut

Preheat oven to 350° F. In large bowl, cream butter, cream cheese and sugar. (Lightly spoon flour into measuring cup; level off.) Stir in remaining ingredients until mixed. Drop by rounded teaspoonful, 2 inches apart, onto ungreased cookie sheets. Bake 15 to 20 minutes until lightly browned.

3 dozen cookies

TIP: Drop by half-teaspoonsful for 5 to 6 dozen dainty, tea-size cookies.

HIGH ALTITUDE: — above 3500 Feet: Reduce baking powder to 1 teaspoon. Bake at 350° F. 15 to 20 minutes.

PARTY PUNCHES

For serving large groups with little fuss or bother, nothing beats punch (either alcoholic or nonalcoholic). One thing to serve…one kind of glass…and almost everything is do-ahead. It's especially good for budget-minded entertaining. A lot will go a long way.

In the good old summertime, serve up frosty tinkling glasses of something colorful and refreshing. On chilly winter days, a steaming cup of something hot and vigorous warms the body and the heart.

Keep in mind the conditions of the room as well as the outdoor temperature when selecting your beverages. No matter how cold it is outside, if the room will be fairly crowded with people for a long period of time, a thoughtful hostess will provide a cooler drink.

Punch will lose its "punch" if not served very cold or very hot. When serving cold punches, chill all the ingredients before mixing and keep the punch cold before and during serving. Add carbonated beverages just before serving; mix only enough to blend, so the carbonation is not lost.

Any form of ice — cubed, cracked, crushed, or molded — will make your beverage look cool and refreshing and help it stay that way. Ice trays and shaped gelatin molds can be used to freeze flavored cubes or "chunks" of ice. Try fruit juices, carbonated beverages, or make decorative ice cubes that have citrus fruit sections, strawberries, cherries or mint leaves frozen in them. Distilled water gives better clarity.

To mold fruit in ice, fill mold or ice cube tray with about ½ inch of water. Arrange fruits on top; freeze. Add more water to cover; freeze again. Use the cubes in glasses; invert and float molds in punch bowl.

For hot punches, float lemon or orange slices with cinnamon sticks in centers or wedges studded with cloves. To help keep the punch hot, serve in large chafing dish or crock pot. If you use a punch bowl make sure it is heat resistant before adding the hot punch. It will help to warm the bowl with hot water before you add the punch.

AMOUNT TO SERVE

How much to serve depends on the kind of party and the number of people. If the party precedes a dinner, two or three punch cups per person is sufficient. If the party is to take the larger part of the afternoon or evening, you had better plan on 4 or 5 punch cups per person. Plan on ½-cup servings for "punch bowl" punches.

Punch Planning Guide

No. of People	Before Dinner	Party
4	1-1½ qt.	2-2½ qt.
6	1½-2 qt.	3-4 qt.
8	2-3 qt.	1-1½ gal.
12	1-1½ gal.	1½-2 gal.
20	1½-2 gal.	2½-3 gal.
50	3-4½ gal.	6-7½ gal.

A chilled punch that's prepared right in the punch bowl just before guests arrive.

CLARET PUNCH

    2 quarts claret wine, chilled
    1 cup Cointreau
    1 cup brandy
    6-oz. can frozen lemonade
        concentrate, thawed
    1 quart club soda, chilled
        Ice cubes or ice mold
    1 orange, sliced

In large punch bowl, combine claret, Cointreau, brandy, frozen lemonade and club soda. Add ice or ice mold. Float orange slices on top.

30 (½ cup) servings

A hot punch – delicious and easy for small gatherings or large groups.

ROSY GLOW CRANBERRY PUNCH

	14 servings	28 servings	42 servings
Sugar	⅓ cup	⅔ cup	1 cup
Nutmeg	¼ teaspoon	½ teaspoon	¾ teaspoon
Cinnamon	¼ teaspoon	½ teaspoon	¾ teaspoon
Salt	¼ teaspoon	½ teaspoon	¾ teaspoon
Water	2½ cups	5 cups	7½ cups
Lemon juice	½ cup	1 cup	1½ cups
Cranberry juice cocktail	4 cups (1 qt.)	8 cups (2 qts.)	12 cups (3 qts.)

In large saucepan, combine all ingredients; mix well. Simmer 10 to 15 minutes. Serve hot in mugs with orange slices floating on top or with cinnamon sticks as stirrers.

½ cup servings

POINTS FOR PERFECT PARTY SANDWICHES

Trim the crusts from bread.

Cut the bread early in the day; cover with a damp towel and refrigerate.

Make fancy shapes with cookie cutter, if desired.

Make fillings a day or two ahead and refrigerate.

"Butter" the bread so filling does not soak into bread. Be sure to cream butter (or margarine) so it spreads easily.

If the filling includes mayonnaise or salad dressing, use a minimum amount of dressing so it will not soak into the bread or separate.

A few hours in advance, fill sandwiches; cover with a damp towel and refrigerate.

Cream cheese fillings have tendency to dry and crack if not well-wrapped.

Allow 3 to 4 tiny sandwiches or 2 to 3 larger sandwiches per guest.

Be sure to chill sandwiches in the refrigerator for at least one hour (longer time is better); this makes it easier to cut these tiny sandwiches.

For neater sandwiches, freeze bread first. Cut and spread while frozen.

Allow plenty of time to make; they take time — but are worth it.

PARTY SANDWICHES

Imagination is unlimited when it comes to party sandwiches. These dainty treats can be open or closed, simple or elaborate.

Party sandwiches can be made from sandwich bread or quick breads. The "sandwich bread" type always has the crust removed, and shapes range from pinwheels, lilies and fancy cutouts to whatever shape you prefer — crescents, triangles, circles, squares and fingers.

Open-faced sandwiches made from quick breads are similar to the kind just described but do not need the crusts removed. They, too, can be made in almost any shape desired.

The real excitement is in the wide range of spreads and garnishes.

To serve, group the sandwiches in a simple design on round or oblong trays or plates. Avoid crowding to facilitate easier serving.

FANCY QUICK BREAD SANDWICHES

For pretty circle slices, save your soup cans. Bake quick bread batter in greased and floured soup cans. One Pillsbury quick bread mix yields 4 individual round loaves from soup cans.

Fruit and nut quick breads lend themselves very nicely to cookie-cutter shaping. Cut your favorite shapes; spread with a cheese spread and garnish.

GARNISHES

(Try one or more of these garnishes on your party sandwiches. If desired, hold in place with a toothpick.)

Olives, sliced or chopped
Celery (strips and leaves)
Carrots (curls)
Pickles (fans)
Raw cauliflower
Pickled beets
Jellied cranberry sauce, cut into slices with canapé cutter
Pineapple chunks
Pimento
Pepper rings (thin)
Nuts, whole, halved or chopped
Lemon wedges or twists
Lime wedges or twists
Watercress
Parsley
Tomatoes (roses or thin slices)
Asparagus tips
Hard cooked eggs (yolk sieved or whole egg sliced)
Radishes

BUTTER SPREADS

Cream ½ cup softened butter or margarine until smooth; add one or more of the following, mixing well:

- catsup or chili sauce, onion, salt
- chopped chives or parsley
- garlic or onion salt or powder
- seasoned salt
- honey
- cinnamon, nutmeg
- any snappy cheese spread
- minced onion

EASY CHEESE SPREADS

Use any prepared pasteurized process cheese spread, softened. If necessary, thin with a few drops milk or cream. Garnish as desired.

Examples are:
pasteurized process Cheddar cheese spread
pasteurized process cheese spread with pimento
pasteurized process cheese spread with bacon

CREAMY PIMENTO SPREAD

   8-oz. pkg. cream cheese, softened
   2 tablespoons milk or cream
   ¼ teaspoon Worcestershire sauce
   Dash salt
   ½ cup (2 oz.) shredded Cheddar cheese
   2 tablespoons chopped pimento

In small bowl, combine cream cheese, milk, Worcestershire sauce and salt; beat until light and fluffy. Fold in cheese and pimento.

1½ cups

PARTY SANDWICH LOAF

   1 loaf white or whole wheat sandwich bread, unsliced
   ½ cup butter or margarine, softened
   3 sandwich fillings (See below)
   2 pkg. (8 oz. each) cream cheese, softened
   ½ cup light cream
   Cucumber or olive slices, to garnish

Trim crusts from bread. Cut lengthwise into 4 slices. Spread 3 slices with butter; then spread each with a different filling. Stack slices, placing unspread slice on top. In large bowl, blend cream cheese and cream until fluffy and soft enough to spread; frost sides and top of loaf. Garnish. For ease in slicing, chill several hours.

1 loaf

TIPS: About 1 cup filling is needed for each layer.

   Filling combinations that taste good together:

   — chicken salad, pineapple cheese filling, ham salad

   — deviled ham-olive filling, peanut butter-honey, egg salad

   Sandwich loaf can be made with alternating white and whole wheat slices. Use remaining slices for a second sandwich loaf or other party sandwiches.

   A few drops of food coloring can be added to cream cheese frosting.

   If loaf is to be refrigerated longer than 2 hours, cover to prevent drying.

HAM SALAD FILLING

   1 cup (8 oz.) ground cooked ham
   2 tablespoons mayonnaise or salad dressing
   1 to 2 tablespoons pickle relish
   1 tablespoon minced onion

In small bowl, combine all ingredients; mix well.

1 cup

TIP: Ground canned luncheon meat may be substituted for ham.

CHICKEN SALAD FILLING

   5-oz. can (¾ cup) cooked chicken, drained and chopped
   ⅓ cup finely chopped celery
   2 tablespoons mayonnaise or salad dressing
   2 tablespoons chopped pimento
   Dash salt or seasoned salt

In small bowl, combine all ingredients; mix well.

1 cup

PINEAPPLE-CHEESE FILLING

   5-oz. jar pasteurized process cheese spread
   ¼ cup drained, crushed pineapple

In small bowl, combine cheese and pineapple; mix well.

¾ cup

PEANUT BUTTER-HONEY SPREAD

   ¾ cup chunky peanut butter
   2 tablespoons honey

In small bowl, combine peanut butter and honey; mix well.

¾ cup

EGG SALAD FILLING

   3 hard-cooked eggs, chopped
   1 tablespoon finely chopped onion or 1 teaspoon instant minced onion
   ½ teaspoon salt or seasoned salt
   1 tablespoon mayonnaise or salad dressing
   2 teaspoons pickle relish

In small bowl, combine all ingredients; mix well.

1 cup

DEVILED HAM-OLIVE FILLING

4½-oz. can (½ cup) deviled ham or ground cooked ham
¼ cup chopped, stuffed green olives
2 tablespoons mayonnaise or salad dressing

In small bowl, combine all ingredients; mix well.

¾ cup

SNACK CREAM PUFFS

¼ cup butter or margarine
½ cup hot water
½ cup Pillsbury's Best All Purpose or Unbleached Flour
¼ teaspoon salt
2 eggs

Preheat oven to 425° F. In medium saucepan, combine butter and water. Bring to boil. (Lightly spoon flour into measuring cup; level off.) Add flour and salt all at once. Cook over medium heat, stirring constantly, until mixture leaves sides of pan and forms a stiff ball. Remove from heat. Blend in eggs, one at a time, beating vigorously after each. Drop by teaspoonful onto ungreased cookie sheet. Bake 13 to 17 minutes until golden brown and crisp. Cool and split. Fill with Crab Salad or other desired filling.

3 to 3½ dozen snacks

TIPS: Cream puffs and filling can be prepared ahead; fill shortly before serving.

About 3 cups of filling are needed to fill 40 puffs.

HIGH ALTITUDE: No change.

CRAB SALAD FILLING

2 cups (two 7½-oz. cans) drained and flaked crabmeat
¼ cup snipped parsley
½ cup finely chopped celery
6 tablespoons mayonnaise or salad dressing
1 teaspoon lemon juice
½ teaspoon paprika
⅛ teaspoon salt or seasoned salt

In medium bowl, combine all ingredients; mix well.

3 cups

TIP: If desired, substitute 2 cups (two 6½-oz. cans) drained and flaked tuna for crabmeat.

SHRIMP-STUFFED CELERY

4½-oz. can (1 cup) tiny or broken shrimp, drained
¼ cup salad dressing or mayonnaise
¼ cup well-drained, crushed pineapple
1 to 2 teaspoons finely chopped green onion or chives
1 teaspoon lemon juice
Dash Tabasco sauce
1 tablespoon chopped nuts
¼ teaspoon salt
6 to 7 stalks celery, cut into 3-inch pieces

In small bowl, combine all ingredients except celery; mix well. Spoon about 2 teaspoons mixture into each celery piece. If desired, garnish with paprika or additional sliced onion or chopped chives.

24 to 28 pieces

TIP: To make ahead, prepare, cover and refrigerate up to 4 hours before serving. Or prepare filling, cover and refrigerate up to 24 hours; fill each celery piece a few hours before serving, cover and refrigerate until served.

FROSTED DATE LOAF

1 pkg. Pillsbury Date Bread Mix
1 egg
1 cup water
3-oz. pkg. cream cheese, softened
3 tablespoons well drained crushed pineapple
8-oz. pkg. cream cheese, softened
2 tablespoons milk
Pecan halves, to garnish

Prepare date bread mix with egg and water. Bake as directed on package. Cool completely. Slice horizontally into 3 layers. In small bowl, combine 3-oz. pkg. of cream cheese and pineapple. Spread filling between layers; stack. In small bowl, combine 8-oz. pkg. of cream cheese and milk; beat until fluffy. Frost sides and top of loaf. Garnish with pecan halves. For ease in slicing, chill loaf for several hours. Cut into ½-inch slices.

12 to 14 slices

TIP: If loaf is prepared the day before, wrap in plastic wrap to prevent frosting from cracking; store in refrigerator.

HIGH ALTITUDE: Follow package directions.

Snack Cream Puffs
Frosted Date Loaf

SMOKED SALMON ROLLS

2 pkg. (3 oz. each) cream
cheese, softened
¼ cup capers
½ pound sliced smoked salmon

Blend cheese with capers. Spread
on salmon. Roll up, jelly roll
fashion. Chill. Cut into ½-inch
slices. Serve on cocktail picks.

40 slices

OLIVE CREAM CHEESE BALL

8-oz. pkg. cream cheese,
softened
⅓ cup chopped stuffed green
olives
¼ cup chopped ripe olives
¼ cup finely chopped onion or
1 tablespoon instant minced
onion
¼ teaspoon Tabasco sauce
½ cup snipped parsley

In medium bowl, combine softened
cream cheese with olives, onions
and Tabasco; mix thoroughly.
Refrigerate cheese mixture about 15
minutes for easier handling. Shape
into ball; roll in parsley to coat
well. Return to refrigerator; chill 15
to 20 minutes or until serving
time. Serve with assorted crackers
or chips.

4-inch ball

Olive Cream Cheese Ball

Casual Entertaining

When the invitation reads, "Come casually," we all look forward to a comfortable, informal get-together. There are many reasons why Americans are choosing this type of entertaining over stuffy, sit-in-the-parlor parties—more working homemakers, busier schedules for the whole family, inflation and the desire to dispense with the unnecessary frills of a bygone era in favor of streamlined suppers. Although the atmosphere is relaxed, there is no reason why the menu cannot be just as imaginative and distinctive as if it were planned for an elaborate setting. "Casual" does not automatically mean hamburgers on the grill. Just glance through the suggested menus and share some of our secrets for unique, informal entertaining—around the fire, the tailgate of a station wagon, a fondue pot or a steaming tureen of homemade soup. These gatherings are especially popular with young people who have little in the way of formal table service. Why, almost anything goes, right down to colorful paper plates, just as long as the party perks with tasty dishes, congenial guests and most important of all—gracious, carefree hosts!

Sunday night and the "gang's all here." They can hardly wait to dip the ladle into one of your fragrant homemade soups and slice off some of that savory hot-from-the-oven bread. Why not serve the soups in mugs for comfortable handling and have the garnishes in bowls near-by for easy access? Set the bread loaves on cutting boards with a bread knife handy. Contrast makes the menu especially interesting with totally different types of soup and bread. If dessert is desired, keep it light—no need for anything hearty or elaborate. Try these recipe favorites for a trim-the-tree party or after a harvest time square dance in your basement or garage.

"Soup's On" Supper
Creole Gumbo
Pumpkin Soup
Onion Casserole Bread
Rye Beer Bread
Cheese Butter
Bleu Cheese Butter

CREOLE GUMBO
2 medium stalks celery, chopped
1 small onion, chopped
½ cup chopped green pepper
2 tablespoons olive or cooking oil
1 clove garlic, minced
1½ teaspoons salt
1 tablespoon Worcestershire sauce
2 cups (16-oz. can) tomatoes
8-oz. can tomato sauce
10-oz. pkg. frozen okra, partially thawed and cut into ½-inch pieces
1 cup (4½-oz. can) shrimp, cut into pieces
1 cup (7½-oz. can) crab meat, flaked
¼ cup dry sherry, if desired
1 tablespoon snipped parsley

In large saucepan, cook celery, onion and green pepper in oil until tender. Stir in garlic, salt, Worcestershire sauce, tomatoes and tomato sauce. Cover and simmer 45 to 60 minutes. Add remaining ingredients. Continue simmering, covered, 15 to 20 minutes until okra is tender. If desired, top with garlic-flavored croutons.

6 to 8 (1 cup) servings

A hollowed-out pumpkin makes a most attractive serving container.

PUMPKIN SOUP

4 cups cubed raw pumpkin, peeled
¼ cup butter or margarine
¼ cup water
2 carrots, cut into pieces
4 cups chicken stock
2 stalks celery, cut into pieces
1 medium onion, quartered
3 sprigs parsley or 1 tablespoon parsley flakes
½ bay leaf
¼ teaspoon powdered thyme
½ cup dry white wine or sherry
1 teaspoon salt
Pepper

In large saucepan, cook pumpkin in butter a few minutes. Add water and carrots; cover and simmer 30 minutes or until pumpkin is tender. Simmer remaining ingredients in another covered saucepan 30 minutes. Strain to remove celery and onion. Process pumpkin and carrots in blender until smooth. Stir in broth. Heat to serving temperature.

6 to 8 (1 cup) servings

TIP: If desired, use 2 cups (16-oz. can) cooked pumpkin. Omit first cooking of pumpkin. After cooking and straining broth, add to pumpkin and continue as directed.

Pumpkin Soup
Rye Beer Bread, p. 44
Creole Gumbo, p. 41
Onion Casserole Bread
Soup Garnishes

ONION CASSEROLE BREAD

1 pkg. Pillsbury Hot Roll Mix
½ cup very warm water (105°-115°F.)
2 eggs (reserve 1 egg white)
¾ cup creamed cottage cheese
1 envelope (1.25 oz.) dry onion soup mix
Onion salt

In large bowl, dissolve yeast from hot roll mix in water. Stir in egg and egg yolk. Add flour mixture, cottage cheese and dry soup mix. Stir until combined. Cover; let rise in warm place until light and doubled in size, 45 to 60 minutes Stir about 20 strokes. Turn into greased (not oiled) 1½-quart casserole. Beat reserved egg white until frothy; brush over surface of dough. Sprinkle with onion salt. Let rise in warm place until light and doubled in size, 30 to 45 minutes. Preheat oven to 350°F. Bake 25 to 35 minutes until golden brown. Immediately remove from pan.

1 loaf

TIP: Warm cottage cheese before adding to speed up rising.

HIGH ALTITUDE—above 3500 Feet: Watch rising times carefully. Bake at 375°F. 25 to 30 minutes.

GARNISHES FOR SOUPS

Top bowls of soup with one of these ideas; select flavors to complement the flavor of the soup:

Croutons, cheese crackers, crushed potato chips, shoestring potatoes, chow mein noodles, popcorn, pretzels.

Shredded cheese, grated Parmesan cheese, crumbled bleu cheese, toasted almonds, crumbled cooked bacon, sieved egg yolk, sliced wieners, chopped peanuts, sour cream, yogurt.

Chopped chives, sliced green onions, sliced radishes, chopped dill pickle, sliced cucumber, green pepper strips, chopped celery tops, shredded carrots, sliced water chestnuts, sliced lemon, sliced avocado.

BLEU CHEESE BUTTER

½ cup butter or margarine, softened
⅓ cup bleu cheese, crumbled
1 tablespoon chopped chives

Cream butter. Add remaining ingredients; mix thoroughly. Serve at room temperature for easier spreading.

¾ cup

A slice of homemade bread topped with a hearty spread—what could be better?

CHEESE BUTTER

½ cup butter or margarine, softened
1 cup (4 oz.) shredded Cheddar or American cheese
½ teaspoon garlic salt
½ teaspoon prepared mustard
½ teaspoon Worcestershire sauce
Dash Tabasco sauce

Cream butter. Add remaining ingredients; blend well. Serve at room temperature for easier spreading.

1¼ cups

RYE BEER BREAD

    3 cups Pillsbury's Best
      All Purpose or
      Unbleached Flour
    2 pkg. active dry yeast
    2 teaspoons salt
    2 cups (16-oz. can) beer
      or water
    ½ cup molasses
    6 tablespoons butter or
      margarine
    3 to 3½ cups Pillsbury's
      Best Rye Flour

(Lightly spoon flour into measuring cup; level off.) In large bowl, combine 2 cups flour, yeast and salt. In saucepan, heat beer, molasses and butter until very warm (120° to 130°F.). Stir into flour mixture. Beat 2 minutes at medium speed. By hand, stir in remaining flour and rye flour to form a stiff dough. On well-floured surface, knead dough until smooth and elastic, 5 to 10 minutes. Place in greased bowl. Cover; let rise in warm place until light and doubled in size, 50 to 60 minutes. Generously grease (not oil) two 9x5 or 8x4-inch loaf pans. Punch down dough; divide and shape into 2 loaves. Place in greased pans. Cover; let rise in warm place until doubled in size, 30 to 45 minutes. Preheat oven to 375°F. Bake 25 to 35 minutes until deep golden brown and loaves sound hollow when lightly tapped. Remove from pans. Cool.

2 loaves

TIP: May shape 2 round hearth loaves and bake on greased cookie sheets.

HIGH ALTITUDE—above 3500 Feet: Let rise just until double in size; watch carefully.

Tailgating Time

Tomato Noggins
Vegetable Dipper Dilly Dip
Hearty Bunwiches
Deviled Eggs
Choco-Date Cake

"Have food—will travel" is the byword of thousands of enthusiastic tailgating fans across the country. Their "movable feast" can be as elegant as cold chicken, imported cheeses and crackers and chilled champagne. But, more likely, the food is as casual as the mood and geared for lumberjack appetites and simple serving and clean-up. This particular menu is especially versatile because it is as appealing at brunch as it is at high noon or right on through to the late supper hours. If weather is warm, substitute a cold, spiced tomato drink for the hot Noggins and presto—you're all set with a summer special. Pass the vegetable tray early to appease appetites while the bacon is grilling or save it for a salad. It's all delicious, and the toting is easy.

TOMATO NOGGINS

    46-oz. can (5½ cups)
      tomato juice
    2 cans (10½ oz. each)
      beef broth
    1 to 2 lemons, sliced

In large saucepan, combine first two ingredients. Heat. Serve in mugs garnished with lemon slices.

8 (1 cup) servings

TIPS: 3 cubes or teaspoons beef bouillon and 2½ cups water can be used for beef broth.

    May add 2 tablespoons (1 oz.) vodka to each cup just before serving.

VEGETABLE DIPPER DILLY DIP

    1½ cups dairy sour cream
    1½ cups mayonnaise or
      salad dressing
    2 tablespoons snipped
      parsley
    2 tablespoons minced
      green onion
    4 teaspoons dill weed
    2 teaspoons Beau Monde
      seasoning

In bowl, combine all ingredients; mix well. Chill several hours. Serve with vegetable dippers such as carrots, zucchini, celery, cucumber or rutabaga.

3 cups

HEARTY BUNWICHES

8 slices (12 oz.) Canadian
   bacon or ham
8 hamburger buns
8 slices pasteurized
   process cheese
8 tomato slices

Grill Canadian bacon slices 3 to 4 inches from hot coals, for 3 to 4 minutes on each side. Toast hamburger buns; top with cheese slices, tomato slices and Canadian bacon. Heat until cheese melts. Serve hot.

8 sandwiches

DEVILED EGGS

6 hard-cooked eggs
½ teaspoon dry mustard
   or 1 teaspoon prepared
   mustard
¼ teaspoon salt
   Dash pepper
¼ cup chopped ripe olives,
   if desired
3 tablespoons
   mayonnaise or salad
   dressing
1 teaspoon vinegar
¼ teaspoon
   Worcestershire sauce,
   if desired
   Paprika

Cool hard-cooked eggs; shell and halve lengthwise. Carefully lift out yolks and place in bowl. Mash yolks with fork and add remaining ingredients except paprika; mix until fluffy. Fill egg whites with yolk mixture. Sprinkle with paprika.

1 dozen deviled eggs

TIP: 1 teaspoon chopped chives, pickle relish, green onions, green olives or ¼ teaspoon curry powder may be added.

Great for potlucks and lunch boxes, too!

CHOCO-DATE CAKE

8-oz. pkg. (1½ cups)
   chopped dates
1½ teaspoons soda
2 cups boiling water
2¾ cups Pillsbury's Best
   All Purpose or
   Unbleached Flour
1½ cups sugar
1½ teaspoons salt
2 tablespoons
   unsweetened cocoa
1 teaspoon vanilla
¾ cup solid shortening or
   margarine, softened
3 eggs
6-oz. pkg. (1 cup)
   semi-sweet chocolate
   pieces
½ cup chopped nuts

In large bowl, combine dates and soda. Pour boiling water over mixture; cool 5 minutes. Grease (not oil) and flour 12-cup fluted tube pan (non-stick finish pan, too). Preheat oven to 350°F. (325°F. for colored pan). (Lightly spoon flour into measuring cup; level off.) Into date mixture, blend remaining ingredients except chocolate pieces and nuts. Beat 3 minutes at medium speed, scraping bowl occasionally. Stir in chocolate pieces and nuts. Pour into prepared pan. Bake 60 to 70 minutes until toothpick inserted in center comes out clean. Cool upright in pan 5 minutes; turn onto serving plate. Cool. Sprinkle with powdered sugar or serve warm cake slices topped with whipped cream.

10-inch ring cake

TIP: For 13x9-inch cake, make cake as directed except reserve ½ cup each chocolate pieces and ¼ cup nuts. Pour batter into prepared pan; sprinkle with reserved chocolate pieces and nuts. Bake 35 to 45 minutes.

HIGH ALTITUDE—above 3500 Feet: Decrease soda to 1 teaspoon; decrease sugar to 1⅓ cups. Bake at 375°F. for 55 to 65 minutes.

For after skiing, skating, trick-or-treating, caroling or anytime a simple but cozy supper sounds inviting, just bring out the steaming bowls of hot, spicy chili. This menu is easily increased to feed a crowd and it's so good everyone will clamor for seconds. Add color and variety by setting out some chili go-togethers—grated Cheddar, chopped onion, diced green pepper, chopped green chilies and/or sour cream. Let the guests help themselves. The almond-frosted bars offer a cooling change of pace from the chili and may be served with a platter of fresh fruit or ice cream balls, if desired.

Spicy Chili Supper
Easy Chili
Cheese Burst Biscuits
Lettuce Wedges-Italian Style
Frosted Cinnamon Bars

Make ahead so flavors will blend.

EASY CHILI
 1 pound ground beef
 1 medium onion, sliced
 ½ cup (1 medium) chopped green pepper
 2 cups (16-oz. can) tomatoes
 4 cups (two 16-oz. cans) undrained red kidney beans
 1 cup (8-oz. can) tomato sauce
 2 to 2½ teaspoons chili powder
 1 teaspoon salt
1½ teaspoons prepared mustard
 1 clove garlic or ⅛ teaspoon garlic powder

In large fry pan or saucepan, brown ground beef; drain. Add remaining ingredients. Simmer uncovered for 1 hour, stirring occasionally. Remove garlic clove before serving. Garnish with crushed corn chips or grated Cheddar cheese, if desired.

6 (1 cup) servings

TIP: Toothpick inserted in garlic clove makes it easier to remove.

CHEESE BURST BISCUITS
10-oz. can Hungry Jack® Refrigerated Big Flaky Biscuits
Ten ½-inch cubes (1.5 oz.) American or Cheddar cheese
 Milk
 Sesame, caraway or poppy seed

Preheat oven to 400°F. Separate biscuit dough into 10 biscuits. Insert cheese cube between layers of each biscuit; seal edges well. Cut deep "X" on the top of biscuit. Brush with milk. Sprinkle with sesame seed. Bake on ungreased cookie sheet 10 to 12 minutes until golden bown. Serve warm.

10 biscuits

LETTUCE WEDGES-ITALIAN STYLE
 ¾ cup dairy sour cream
 ⅓ cup mayonnaise or salad dressing
 ½ to 1 pkg. Italian salad dressing mix
 ¼ cup water
 1 teaspoon sugar
 ⅛ teaspoon salt
 1 medium head lettuce, cut into 6 wedges
2½-oz. jar sliced mushrooms, drained

Combine all ingredients except lettuce and mushrooms. Mix well. Spoon dressing over lettuce wedges. Top with mushrooms.

6 servings

A sweet, pat-in-the-pan crumb crust is the base for this cake-like bar. The almond-flavored frosting makes a delicious topping.

FROSTED CINNAMON BARS

2 cups Pillsbury's Best
  All Purpose or
  Unbleached Flour
1¼ cups sugar
¼ cup firmly packed
  brown sugar
½ cup butter or
  margarine, softened
½ cup chopped nuts
1 teaspoon soda
1 teaspoon cinnamon
¾ teaspoon salt
1 cup buttermilk or sour
  milk*
1 teaspoon vanilla
1 egg
Frosting
2 cups powdered sugar
3 to 4 tablespoons milk
  or light cream
¼ teaspoon almond
  extract or vanilla

Preheat oven to 350°F. (Lightly spoon flour into measuring cup; level off.) In large bowl, combine first four ingredients; blend at low speed until crumbly. Press 2 cups crumb mixture into ungreased 13x9-inch pan. To remaining crumb mixture, add nuts, soda, cinnamon, salt, buttermilk, vanilla and egg; blend well. Pour evenly over crumb mixture. Bake 20 to 25 minutes until toothpick inserted in center comes out clean. Cool 20 minutes. In small bowl, blend Frosting ingredients until smooth. Spread over partially cooled bars. Cool completely; cut into bars.

2 to 3 dozen bars

*To sour milk, use 1 tablespoon vinegar plus enough milk to make 1 cup.

HIGH ALTITUDE: No change.

Lettuce Wedge Italian Style

It's great fun, now and then, to revive this craze of the 60s and treat yourself to a do-it-yourself supper around the bubbling fondue pot. Fondue suppers are take-your-time meals which are relaxing for the guests and super-easy for the hostess, even after a day at the office! Give your guests plenty of elbow room at the table and provide essential platters of "fixings" for easy reaching, especially if you are serving over four people. And, of course, everyone should be cautious around the hot oil or cheese so that no one gets burned or tips over the pot. You will want to save your special table linens for another occasion because there is bound to be some splattering.

Beef should be at room temperature before cooking to help keep splattering to a minimum.

BEEF FONDUE

2 pounds boneless sirloin or tenderloin, cut into 1-inch cubes
Sauces (See below)
Cooking oil

Arrange cubes of meat in individual dishes or a large serving dish (line with lettuce leaves, if desired). Set out 3 to 4 sauces. Place fondue pot in center of table. Heat cooking oil to 375° F. or until it browns a cube of bread quickly. Each guest

Fun With Fondue
Beef Fondue
with Sauces and Butters
OR
Swiss Cheese Fondue
Green Goddess Salad
Crescent Onion Bread
Fruit Fondue au Rum
OR
Chocolate Fondue Sauce

uses fondue fork to spear meat and then cooks in hot oil until of desired doneness. Remove to plate and eat with dinner fork (the fondue fork becomes very hot in the oil), dipping into desired sauces. For an added treat, pass a bowl of chopped salted peanuts along with the sauces.

4 servings

TIPS: Try other types of fondue — use cubes of lamb (serve with chutney, sweet and sour and curry sauces) or fresh or frozen shrimp, thawed and well drained (serve with cocktail, sweet and sour, or curry sauces).

Whole fresh mushrooms or cubes of raw eggplant may be added to dishes of meat. Each guest cooks vegetable along with meat.

If oil becomes too cool, place on range for a few minutes to reheat.

Strain leftover oil and store in refrigerator; use for fondue again.

A variety of sauces for dipping should be available. Try bottled steak sauces, horseradish sauce, cocktail dips, mustard sauce, teriyaki sauce, or bleu cheese salad dressing; or try making your own sauces. Below are some of our favorites.

CURRY SAUCE

½ cup dairy sour cream
½ teaspoon curry powder
⅛ teaspoon salt
Dash Tabasco sauce

Combine all ingredients; mix well. Refrigerate until serving time.

½ cup

HOT CATSUP SAUCE

½ cup catsup
1½ teaspoons vinegar
½ teaspoon prepared horseradish
Dash Tabasco sauce

Combine all ingredients; mix well. Refrigerate until serving time.

½ cup

ZIPPY STEAK BUTTER

    6 tablespoons butter or
        margarine, softened
    ¼ teaspoon salt
    ½ teaspoon dry mustard, if
        desired
    2 teaspoons lemon juice
    1 teaspoon Worcestershire
        sauce
        Dash pepper

Cream butter; blend in
remaining ingredients, mixing
well. Let stand at room
temperature until serving time.

½ cup

*Prepare cheese fondue just before
serving because it is best when eaten
immediately. The cheese-flour
mixture can be prepared ahead of
time to make last minute
preparation easy.*

SWISS CHEESE FONDUE

    1 clove garlic
    ¾ cup sauterne or Chablis
        white wine
    3 cups (12 oz.) shredded
        natural Swiss cheese
    2 tablespoons flour
    ⅛ teaspoon nutmeg
    ¼ teaspoon salt
        Dash pepper
    1 to 2 tablespoons kirsch, if
        desired
    1 loaf French bread, cut into
        bite-size pieces

Rub inside of saucepan or fondue
dish with cut garlic clove. Add
wine and heat until bubbly.
Combine cheese, flour, nutmeg,
salt and pepper. Add about ¼
cup of cheese mixture to wine;
stir vigorously. Continue adding
cheese in small amounts and
stirring until all cheese is melted
and mixture is thoroughly
blended. Stir in kirsch. Keep hot
while serving. Each guest uses
fondue fork to dip bread into
fondue.

4 to 5 servings

TIP: If fondue becomes too thick
during serving, stir in a little
more warm wine.

GREEN GODDESS SALAD

    1 clove garlic
    1 quart romaine lettuce
    2 cups head lettuce
    2 cups leaf spinach
Dressing
    ½ clove garlic, crushed
    ½ cup mayonnaise or salad
        dressing
    ¼ cup dairy sour cream
    ½ to 1 can (2 oz.) anchovy
        fillets, chopped
    2 tablespoons snipped parsley
    1 tablespoon chopped green
        onion
    1 tablespoon tarragon vinegar
    1 tablespoon lemon juice
    ¼ teaspoon salt
        Freshly ground pepper
    1 or 2 drops green food
        coloring

Rub salad bowl with cut garlic
clove (use ½ garlic clove in
dressing). Tear greens into bite-size
pieces in bowl. Combine dressing
ingredients; mix well. Just before
serving, pour dressing over greens.
Toss lightly.

4 servings

TIP: If desired, save a few anchovy
fillets for garnish.

*A dandy accompaniment for the Beef
Fondue.*

CRESCENT ONION BREAD

    2 cans (8 oz. each) Pillsbury
        Refrigerated Quick Crescent
        Dinner Rolls
    3 tablespoons instant minced
        onion
    2 tablespoons grated Parmesan
        cheese
    2 tablespoons French dressing
    2 tablespoons butter or
        margarine, melted
    2 teaspoons grated Parmesan
        cheese

Preheat oven to 375° F. Generously
grease (not oil) 8 or 9-inch round
cake or pie pan. Separate each can
crescent dough into 2 large
rectangles; firmly press perforations
to seal. In small bowl, combine
onion, 2 tablespoons Parmesan
cheese and French salad dressing;
spread mixture over each rectangle.
Starting at longer side, roll up;
press edges to seal. Wind dough
into greased pan, beginning at
outer edge and coiling inward. Seal
ends of dough. Bake 15 to 20
minutes until golden brown. Brush
with melted margarine; sprinkle
with 2 teaspoons Parmesan cheese.
Serve warm.

1 loaf

TIP: To reheat, wrap in foil; heat
at 350° F. for 10 to 12 minutes.

HIGH ALTITUDE: No change.

FRUIT FONDUE AU RUM

3 tablespoons butter or
margarine
1½ cups firmly packed brown
sugar
½ cup evaporated milk
2 tablespoons rum or
1 teaspoon rum flavoring

In medium saucepan over low heat, melt butter. Add brown sugar; mix. Gradually stir in milk. Continue beating and stirring constantly until sugar is dissolved. Remove from heat. Let stand about 3 minutes; stir in rum. Serve warm in fondue dish over candlewarmer.

1½ cups

Dippers for Dessert Fondues:
Cubes of angel food or sponge cake
Vanilla wafers
Banana slices
Orange or tangarine sections
Pineapple chunks
Strawberries
Apple or pear pieces
Mandarin oranges
Cherries
Large marshmallows
TIP: Sauce can be made ahead.
Prepare, cover and refrigerate.
Serve cold or reheat.

CHOCOLATE FONDUE SAUCE

2 squares (2 oz.)
unsweetened chocolate
1 tablespoon butter or
margarine
1 cup sugar
5⅜-oz. can (⅔ cup)
evaporated milk

In small saucepan, melt chocolate and butter together over low heat. Add sugar and mix. Gradually stir in milk. Continue heating until sugar is dissolved. Serve in fondue dish over candlewarmer.

1¼ cups

Winter Picnic By The Fire

Cornish Pasties
OR
Ham and Chicken
Crescent Sandwiches
Stuffed Celery
Sour Cream Apple Squares
OR
Chocolate-Topped
Oatmeal Bars
Irish Coffee

Snap out of the mid-winter doldrums and surprise your friends with a napkin-lined, food-filled basket for each person or couple and tuck in a split of wine. Spread beach towels or blankets on the floor in front of a flickering fire and plan an after-supper sing-along. After the endless rounds of dressy dinner and cocktail parties throughout the holiday season, this charming but casual party will be welcomed like a breath of Spring in the middle of January. And happy news for the hostess—the menu is as penny-wise as it is tasty!

This mouth-watering meal-in-a-crust is especially popular in mining areas where the Pasties can be served hot for supper or carried cold in a lunch bucket.

CORNISH PASTIES

1 pound ground beef
1 cup finely cubed,
    uncooked potato
½ cup thinly sliced,
    uncooked carrot
¼ cup chopped celery
1 small onion, chopped
10¾-oz. can condensed
    cream of mushroom
    soup
½ teaspoon salt
¼ teaspoon poultry
    seasoning
Dash pepper
9½-oz. pkg. Pillsbury Pie
    Crust Mix

In fry pan, brown ground beef; drain. Add potatoes, carrots, celery, onion, soup, salt, poultry seasoning and pepper. Mix well. Prepare double pie crust recipe using mix. Divide dough into 6 equal portions. Roll out each portion on a floured surface to a 7-inch circle. Place generous ½ cup meat mixture on each pastry circle. Moisten edges with water; fold in half. Seal edges and prick top with fork. Place on ungreased cookie sheet. Preheat oven to 375°F. Bake pasties 25 to 30 minutes or until light golden brown. Eat from hand like a sandwich or serve with mushroom sauce or beef gravy.

6 pasties

TIPS: Pasties can be assembled several hours ahead and refrigerated until ready to bake.

Two cups finely cubed leftover roast beef may be substituted for ground beef.

HIGH ALTITUDE: No change.

Stuffed Celery, p. 52, Ham and Chicken Crescent Sandwiches, p. 52, Cornish Pasties

A Bake-Off® inspiration and one of our favorites!

HAM AND CHICKEN CRESCENT SANDWICHES

    5-oz. can (¾ cup) cooked chicken, finely chopped
    ¾ cup (3 oz.) shredded Cheddar or American cheese
    ½ cup (2 oz.) finely cubed, cooked ham
    ¼ to ⅓ cup creamy Italian or garlic salad dressing
    8-oz. can Pillsbury Refrigerated Quick Crescent Dinner Rolls
    Sesame seed

Preheat oven to 375°F. Combine first four ingredients; mix well. Separate crescent dough into four rectangles; firmly press perforations to seal. Cut each rectangle in half crosswise; press to 4-inch squares. Spoon about ¼ cup meat mixture onto center of each square. Pull 4 corners of dough to top center of filling; twist slightly and seal edges. Place on ungreased cookie sheet; sprinkle with sesame seed. Bake 15 to 20 minutes until golden brown. Serve immediately.

8 sandwiches

TIP: To make ahead, prepare, cover and refrigerate up to 2 hours; bake as directed.

    To reheat, wrap in foil; heat at 350°F. for 8 to 10 minutes.

HIGH ALTITUDE: No change.

STUFFED CELERY

    3-oz. pkg. cream cheese, softened
    1 teaspoon lemon juice, if desired
    ½ teaspoon Worcestershire sauce
    ¼ teaspoon garlic or onion salt or seasoned salt
    2 to 3 stalks celery

In small bowl, combine all ingredients except celery; blend well. Spoon mixture into celery, using about 2 tablespoons for each stalk. Cut each stalk into 3-inch pieces. Garnish.

6 to 9 pieces

TIP: Use any of these for a garnish: paprika, seasoned salt, pickle relish, chopped or sliced olives, green onion or chives, chopped nuts or lemon curls.

Apples enhanced by sugar and spice.

SOUR CREAM APPLE SQUARES

    2 cups Pillsbury's Best All Purpose or Unbleached Flour*
    2 cups firmly packed brown sugar
    ½ cup butter or margarine, softened
    1 cup chopped nuts
    1 to 2 teaspoons cinnamon
    1 teaspoon soda
    ½ teaspoon salt
    1 cup dairy sour cream
    1 teaspoon vanilla
    1 egg
    2 cups (2 medium) peeled, finely chopped apples

Preheat oven to 350°F. (Lightly spoon flour into measuring cup; level off.) In large bowl, combine first three ingredients; blend at low speed until crumbly. Stir in nuts. Press 2¾ cups crumb mixture into ungreased 13x9-inch pan. To remaining mixture, add cinnamon, soda, salt, sour cream, vanilla and egg; blend well. Stir in apples. Spoon evenly over base. Bake 25 to 35 minutes until toothpick inserted in center comes out clean. Cut into squares.

12 to 15 squares

*If using Pillsbury's Best Self-Rising Flour, omit soda and salt.

HIGH ALTITUDE—above 3500 Feet: Bake at 375°F. for 25 to 35 minutes.

Chocolate and peanut butter once again lead the popularity poll in these easy-to-make bars.

CHOCOLATE-TOPPED OATMEAL BARS

    1 pkg. Pillsbury Coconut Almond or Coconut Pecan Frosting Mix
    3 cups rolled oats
    1 cup solid shortening or margarine, softened
    ½ cup sugar
    6-oz. pkg. (1 cup) semi-sweet chocolate pieces
    ¾ cup peanut butter

Preheat oven to 350°F. In large bowl, blend first four ingredients at low speed until crumbly. Press mixture into ungreased 15x10-inch jelly roll pan or 13x9-inch pan. Bake 15 to 20 minutes until light golden brown. In small saucepan over low heat, combine chocolate pieces and peanut butter. Stir constantly until chocolate pieces are melted. Spread over bars. Chill; cut into bars.

2 to 3 dozen bars

HIGH ALTITUDE: No change.

IRISH COFFEE

Pour 1 to 2 tablespoons Irish whiskey into each warmed serving cup. Add 1 to 2 teaspoons sugar and fill with hot coffee. Top with whipped cream.

Irish Coffee
Chocolate-Topped Oatmeal Bars

Foreign Intrigue

Nowadays, a meal ticket to those "far away places with the strange sounding names" can be readily purchased at the corner grocery store. Italy, France, Germany, etc. — just name your pleasure and plan a party! And the best part?

Preparing the tantalizing specialties of countries across the border or across the sea is often no more difficult than concocting family favorites which are second nature to us. The exotic spices of the Middle and Far East, the delicate sauces of western Europe and the robust favorites of the Irish and

German diets — all these adventures and more await you as you embark upon the edible excursions in this section. Foreign cookery is as festive as it is fun, and certainly your guests will enjoy celebrating with you our rich culinary heritage from many nations.

A Scandinavian patchwork of colors and flavors — traditional yuletide treats from the Land of the Midnight Sun and the home of ruby red lingonberries, yeast breads and flat breads, the full nets of fishermen and bountiful farms. Traditionally, a smorgasbord features a cold table for the chilled and room-temperature foods and a hot table for the main course. You may follow suit or just divide one long table into two serving areas. Usually the cold buffet is left out until dessert is served, so guests may help themselves repeatedly. All dishes are presented decoratively, and garnishes of parsley and dill sprigs, lemon slices and wedges, radish rosettes and lettuce leaves are used to enhance appearances. For a more elaborate feast, you may add the following foods to your menu: sardines, smoked salmon, deviled eggs, a variety of Scandinavian cheeses, additional authentic breads and crackers for the cold table; and ham, pork loin or spareribs, Swedish brown beans and braised red cabbage for the hot table. If lingonberries are available in your

Scandinavian Smorgasbörd

Herring Platter
Lefse
Rye Bread
Swedish Meatballs
Raw-Fried Potatoes
Dilled Peas
Spicy Fruit Soup
Spritz Cookies
Swedish Shortbread

area, they may be made into a simple sauce and served over Swedish pancakes or rice pudding for other dessert ideas.

HERRING PLATTER

The herring platter is served as an appetizer or first course and should be the first item on the

smorgasbord. The most common ingredients are pickled herring chunks, sliced Beet Pickles*, sliced hard-cooked eggs, Cucumbers in Sour Cream*. Arrange them attractively on a platter, using parsley, dill sprigs and lemon slices for garnishes.

*Recipes printed below.

BEET PICKLES

    2 cans (16 oz. each) small whole or sliced beets
    2 cups sugar
    1 cup vinegar
    1 cup water
    ½ lemon, sliced
    ½ teaspoon cinnamon
    ½ teaspoon pepper

Drain beets, reserving 1 cup of liquid. Set aside. In saucepan, combine beet liquid and remaining ingredients; boil 10 minutes. Drop beets into hot liquid. Cool slightly. Place in tightly covered container; refrigerate. Pickles will keep in refrigerator 3 to 4 weeks.

1 quart

CUCUMBERS IN SOUR CREAM

    1 large or 2 medium
      cucumbers, thinly
      sliced
    ½ teaspoon salt
    ½ cup dairy sour cream or
      plain yogurt
    1 tablespoon sugar
    1 tablespoon vinegar
      Pepper

Slice cucumbers into shallow bowl. Sprinkle with salt and let stand about 20 minutes. Drain. Add remaining ingredients and toss lightly. Chill before serving.

3 to 4 servings

TIP: If desired, add chopped or sliced onion with the sour cream. ¼ teaspoon dill weed also makes a good flavor addition.

Orange peel and anise seed add extra flavor to this round loaf. Try caraway seed for a flavor variation.

SCANDINAVIAN RYE BREAD

    1 cup water
    1 cup buttermilk or sour
      milk*
    ¼ cup solid shortening or
      cooking oil
    ¼ cup molasses

    2 cups Pillsbury's Best
      All Purpose or
      Unbleached Flour
    ⅓ cup firmly packed
      brown sugar or honey
    1 tablespoon grated
      orange peel
    3 teaspoons salt
    1 teaspoon anise or
      caraway seed
    ½ teaspoon soda
    2 pkgs. active dry yeast
    4 to 4½ cups Pillsbury's
      Best Medium Rye
      Flour

Heat first four ingredients until very warm (120°-130°F.). (Lightly spoon flour into measuring cup; level off.) In large bowl, combine warm liquid and remaining ingredients except rye flour; beat 3 minutes at medium speed. By hand, stir in enough flour to make a stiff dough. On well-floured surface, knead dough until smooth and elastic, about 5 minutes. Place in greased bowl. Cover; let rise in warm place until light and doubled in size, 45 to 60 minutes. Punch down dough; divide. Shape into 2 round loaves; place on opposite corners of greased (not oiled) cookie sheet. Cover; let rise in warm place until light and doubled in size, 45 to 60 minutes. Preheat oven to 350°F. Bake 45 to 50 minutes until deep golden brown and loaves sound hollow when lightly tapped. If desired, brush warm loaves with melted butter or margarine.

2 round loaves

*To sour milk, use 1 tablespoon vinegar plus enough milk to make 1 cup.

HIGH ALTITUDE: No change.

SWEDISH MEATBALLS

    ¾ pound lean ground beef
    ½ pound ground veal
    ¼ pound ground pork
    1½ cups soft bread crumbs
    ½ cup light cream
    1 tablespoon butter or
      margarine
    ½ cup chopped onion
    1 egg
    ¼ cup snipped parsley
    1½ teaspoons salt
    ⅛ teaspoon ginger
      Dash pepper
      Dash nutmeg
    2 tablespoons butter or
      margarine
    2 tablespoons flour
    1 cup milk

In medium bowl, combine meats; mix well. In small bowl, soak bread crumbs in cream for about 5 minutes. In fry pan, melt butter and add onion; cook until tender. Stir onion, crumbs, egg, parsley and seasonings into meat mixture. Blend about 5 minutes at medium speed. Shape into 1½-inch balls. (Mixture will be soft; for ease in shaping, wet hands or chill mixture.) In small fry pan, melt 2 tablespoons butter; brown meatballs. Shake fry pan to keep balls round; don't overcrowd pan. Remove meatballs. Stir flour into drippings in fry pan. Cook over low heat, stirring until mixture is smooth and bubbly. Remove from heat. Stir in milk. Heat to boiling, stirring constantly. Boil 1 minute. Return meatballs to pan. Cover; cook slowly for 30 minutes.

30 meatballs

LEFSE

1 cup Pillsbury's Best
All Purpose or
Unbleached Flour
3 cups mashed potatoes,
cooled
¼ cup butter or
margarine, melted
1 tablespoon cream
1 teaspoon salt
½ teaspoon baking
powder
½ teaspoon sugar

(Lightly spoon flour into measuring cup; level off.) In bowl, combine all ingredients; mix well. Divide into 20 pieces. Shape each piece into ball; roll with lefse rolling pin or cloth-covered rolling pin into thin circle on floured surface. Bake on moderately hot griddle or lefse baker; do not grease griddle. Bake until lightly flecked with brown; turn and bake other side. If large bubbles form, they should be pierced. Cool on clean towel. Cut in half; fold in half. Wrap to keep from drying out. Store in refrigerator. Serve with butter, sugar or jam.

20 lefse

RAW FRIED POTATOES

6 cups (6 medium) thinly
sliced potatoes
1 tablespoon finely chopped
onion
6 tablespoons butter or
margarine
Salt
Pepper

In fry pan, fry potatoes and onion in butter. Add salt and pepper; continue frying, partially covered, over low heat until bottom has a crisp golden crust and potatoes are tender. Turn and brown other side.

6 servings

Aquavit, the Scandinavian "water of life", is served icy cold with foods such as those on Herring Platter.

DILLED PEAS

2 pkg. (10 oz. each) baby peas frozen in butter sauce
⅔ cup finely chopped onion
2 tablespoons butter or margarine
¼ cup diced pimento
½ teaspoon dill weed

Cook peas as directed on package. In medium saucepan, fry onion in butter until tender. Stir in pimento, dill weed and peas in butter sauce; heat through.

6 servings

SPICY FRUIT SOUP

8 oz. pitted prunes, cut up
4 oz. dried apricots, cut up
½ cup golden raisins
4 cups water
2 cups orange juice
⅓ cup sugar
3 tablespoons quick-cooking tapioca
½ teaspoon salt
3-inch cinnamon stick
6 whole cloves

In large saucepan, combine all ingredients except cinnamon and cloves. Place cinnamon and cloves in teaball or cheesecloth bag; add to fruit mixture. Heat to boiling; reduce heat. Cover and simmer until fruits are tender, about 30 to 40 minutes. Remove cinnamon and cloves. Serve hot or cold.

6 (¾ cup) servings

SPRITZ COOKIES

1 cup butter or margarine, softened
1 cup powdered sugar
1 egg or 2 egg yolks
1 teaspoon vanilla
½ teaspoon almond extract
2⅓ cups Pillsbury's Best All Purpose or Unbleached Flour
½ teaspoon salt

Preheat oven to 400° F. In bowl, cream butter and powdered sugar. Beat in egg, vanilla and almond extract. (Lightly spoon flour into measuring cup; level off.) Stir in flour and salt until well mixed. Press a small amount of dough at a time through a cookie press onto ungreased cookie sheets. Bake 6 to 8 minutes until set but not browned.

6 dozen cookies

HIGH ALTITUDE—above 3500 Feet: Bake at 400° F. 8 to 10 minutes.

SWEDISH SHORTBREAD

1 cup butter or margarine, softened
½ cup plus 2 tablespoons sugar
2 to 2½ cups Pillsbury's Best All Purpose or Unbleached Flour
⅓ cup raspberry jam
1 cup powdered sugar
1 teaspoon almond extract
2 to 3 teaspoons water

Preheat oven to 350° F. (Lightly spoon flour into measuring cup; level off.) In bowl, cream butter and sugar; add flour and mix well. Divide dough into 6 parts. On ungreased cookie sheets, roll or pat each part into a strip about 1½ inches wide and 12 inches long. Using knife handle, make slight indentation lengthwise down center of each strip. Do not make indentation too deep or cookies will break. Fill indentation with jam. Bake 10 to 12 minutes until edges are lightly browned. In small bowl, mix powdered sugar, almond extract and water to make thin glaze. While still warm, drizzle glaze across strips and cut diagonally into 1-inch slices.

5 to 6 dozen cookies

HIGH ALTITUDE: No change.

Although the cuisine of rural Greece is not extensive, it is widely revered for high-quality lamb, olive products, fruits, nuts and wines. The Egg and Lemon Soup is probably the most popular soup of the country, and the Moussaka could rightly be called the national dish. Most Greek salads feature olives and the distinctive feta cheese, a salty, fairly soft white product made from goat's milk. The Greek people are remembered fondly by tourists for their generous hospitality — the perfect accompaniment for their unique style of cooking.

Greek

Egg and Lemon Soup
Moussaka
Greek Tossed Salad
Honey Twist Sweet Bread
Fruit Chews OR
Syrian Nutmeg Cake

This soup is accented with tangy lemon, a common ingredient in Greek cuisine.

EGG AND LEMON SOUP
4 cups chicken broth
4 teaspoons or cubes
   chicken bouillon
⅓ cup white or brown rice
3 eggs
2 tablespoons lemon juice

In large saucepan, combine broth, bouillon and rice. Cover and cook until rice is tender, about 20 minutes (40 minutes for brown rice). Beat eggs well; beat in lemon juice. Slowly blend in half of hot chicken broth; return mixture to saucepan. Heat over low heat until mixture becomes creamy and hot, stirring occasionally; do not boil. (Boiling will cause the mixture to curdle.) Garnish with fresh lemon slices or parsley sprigs.

4 (1-cup) servings

Egg and Lemon Soup

Lean ground beef may be substituted for part or all of the lamb, but it is traditional to use lamb.

MOUSSAKA

- 1 pound ground lamb
- 1 medium onion, chopped
- 1 tablespoon snipped parsley
- 1 teaspoon salt
- 1/8 teaspoon pepper
- 1/8 teaspoon nutmeg
- 16-oz. can (2 cups) tomatoes, drained
- 1/4 cup dry red wine or water
- 1 medium eggplant
- 2 eggs
- 1/4 cup milk
- 1/4 cup grated Parmesan cheese

In fry pan, brown lamb; drain. Add onion, parsley, salt, pepper, nutmeg, tomatoes and wine. Peel eggplant and slice crosswise into 1/4-inch thick slices. Arrange half of eggplant slices in bottom of 8-inch square pan or 1½-quart shallow casserole. Top with half of meat mixture, remaining eggplant slices and remaining meat. Bake at 375°F. 40 minutes until eggplant is tender. Beat eggs and milk together; pour over partially baked casserole. Sprinkle with cheese. Bake 10 to 15 minutes longer until egg mixture is set. Let stand about 10 minutes before serving; cut into squares.

4 servings

This bread can be made pretty as a picture every time. It is easy to make and the honey mixture adds a delicate flavor.

HONEY TWIST SWEET BREAD

- 1 pkg. Pillsbury Hot Roll Mix
- 2/3 cup very warm water (105°-115°F.)
- 1/4 cup sugar
- 2 tablespoons butter or margarine, softened
- 2 eggs (reserve 1 white)

Topping

- 1/4 cup butter or margarine, softened
- 2 tablespoons honey
- 2/3 cup powdered sugar
- Reserved egg white

In large bowl, dissolve yeast from hot roll mix and sugar in water. Stir in 2 tablespoons butter and eggs. Add flour mixture; blend well. Cover; let rise in warm place until light and doubled in size, 45 to 60 minutes. Grease (not oil) 9-inch round cake pan or 10-inch pie pan. On well-floured surface, toss dough until no longer sticky. Shape into long roll about 1-inch in diameter. Wind roll into greased pan, beginning at outer edge and coiling in. Combine Topping ingredients; blend until smooth. Brush half of Topping over dough. Let rise in warm place until light and doubled in size, 30 to 45 minutes. Preheat oven to 375°F. Bake 25 to 30 minutes until golden brown. Brush warm bread with remaining Topping. Cool in pan 10 minutes. Loosen edges; remove from pan.

1 round loaf

HIGH ALTITUDE — above 3500 Feet: Bake at 375°F. for 30 to 35 minutes.

GREEK TOSSED SALAD

- 1/4 cup cooking oil
- 1/4 cup vinegar
- 1/2 teaspoon sugar
- 1/2 teaspoon salt
- 1/8 teaspoon oregano
- 1/8 teaspoon dry mustard
- 1/2 medium head lettuce
- 1/4 green pepper, cut into thin strips
- 1/4 cup pitted ripe olives, sliced
- 1/2 cup (4 oz.) feta cheese, crumbled
- 2 green onions, chopped

In covered jar, combine first six ingredients; shake well. Tear lettuce into bite-size pieces; put in salad bowl. Add remaining ingredients. Just before serving, pour dressing over greens; toss lightly.

3 to 4 servings

A nutritious, moist cookie. Easy and quick to make.

FRUIT CHEWS

- 1 cup dried apricots or figs, cut up
- 1 cup dates, cut up
- 1½ cups raisins
- 1 cup flaked coconut
- 1/2 cup chopped nuts
- 1/4 cup sesame seeds

Grind first three ingredients using food grinder or blender. Mix with coconut and nuts. Form into 1-inch balls. Roll in sesame seeds, pressing seeds firmly into chews.

2½ dozen

TIP: Sesame seeds give nutty flavor if lightly toasted at 350°F. for about 20 minutes. Stir frequently.

Greek Tossed Salad
Moussaka
Honey Twist Sweet Bread

Nutmeg is the intriguing flavor in this cake that's not too sweet for an early morning snack.

SYRIAN NUTMEG CAKE

    2 cups Pillsbury's Best
      All Purpose or
      Unbleached Flour
    2 cups firmly packed
      brown sugar
    ½ cup solid shortening or
      margarine, softened
    ¾ cup chopped nuts
      (reserve ¼ cup for
      topping)
    1 teaspoon soda
    1 teaspoon nutmeg
    1 cup dairy sour cream
    1 egg

Preheat oven to 350°F. (Lightly spoon flour into measuring cup; level off.) In large bowl, combine first three ingredients; blend at low speed until crumbly. Press 2 cups crumb mixture into ungreased 9-inch square pan. To remaining crumb mixture, add ½ cup nuts, soda, nutmeg, sour cream and egg; blend well. Pour batter over crumb mixture. Sprinkle with remaining ¼ cup nuts. Bake 35 to 40 minutes until toothpick inserted in center comes out clean. Serve warm.

9 to 12 squares

HIGH ALTITUDE — above 3500 Feet: Add 2 tablespoons flour and 1 teaspoon baking powder. Reduce sugar to 1½ cups and soda to ½ teaspoon. Bake at 375°F. 35 to 40 minutes.

Oriental

Oriental Spinach Soup
Sukiyaki
Fried Rice
Gingered Sherbet
Almond Sugar Cookies

The mysterious Orient with its exotic culture and cuisine makes a fantastic featured attraction for a special dinner party. The table-side preparation and the serving of food is a delightfully lengthy process which is staged to continue at a leisurely pace throughout the evening. Here, the cook-at-the-table entrée is accented with a delicate soup, traditional fried rice and a light dessert with a surprise ingredient. (Actually, dessert is not an important part of the Oriental meal, but we bow to American custom and include this appropriately refreshing finale.) Ingredients for the Sukiyaki should be sliced or chopped with care and artfully arranged with like foods together for appearance as well as ease in cooking. Why not provide your guests with chopsticks to add to the fun and authenticity of the occasion?

ORIENTAL SPINACH SOUP

    10-oz. pkg. cut leaf
      spinach frozen in
      butter sauce
    10½-oz. can condensed
      chicken broth
    ⅔ cup water
    2 teaspoons cornstarch
    ¼ cup diced celery
    1 tablespoon sliced green
      onions
    1 teaspoon soy sauce

Cook spinach as directed on package. If desired, chill chicken broth; skim off fat. In large saucepan, combine chicken broth, water, cornstarch, celery, onions and soy sauce. Bring to a boil. Reduce heat; simmer 5 minutes. Add spinach in butter sauce. Heat until very warm but not boiling. Garnish with additional sliced green onions.

5 to 6 (½ cup) servings

FRIED RICE

    2 tablespoons chopped
      onion
    2 tablespoons cooking
      oil
    4 cups cooked rice
    2 tablespoons soy sauce
    1 egg, well beaten
    2 tablespoons minced
      parsley
    ⅛ teaspoon pepper

In fry pan, cook onion in oil until tender. Add rice and soy sauce. Cook over low heat 5 to 10 minutes, stirring with a fork occasionally. Add egg, parsley and pepper. Cook over low heat 5 minutes, stirring constantly. If desired, serve with additional soy sauce.

5 to 6 servings

SUKIYAKI

1 to 1½ pounds sirloin tip
   or sirloin steak
2 tablespoons cooking
   oil or shortening
½ cup soy sauce
⅔ cup water
3 tablespoons sugar
½ teaspoon monosodium
   glutamate (MSG), if
   desired
5-oz. can bamboo shoots,
   drained
1 cup green onions,
   cut into 1-inch slices
2 medium onions,
   thinly sliced
16-oz. can bean sprouts,
   drained
5-oz. can water chestnuts,
   sliced
1 cup (8 oz.) sliced,
   fresh mushrooms

Cut meat into paper-thin slices across grain, then into strips 1-inch wide. (Slightly freezing meat makes slicing easier.) In large fry pan or wok, brown strips 2 to 3 minutes in hot oil. Combine soy sauce, water, sugar and MSG; pour over meat. Push meat to one side of fry pan. Keeping ingredients separate, add bamboo shoots, green onions and onion slices. Cook 5 to 10 minutes, turning vegetables frequently. Push vegetables to one side. Add bean sprouts, water chestnuts and mushrooms, keeping ingredients separate. Cook 2 minutes until hot. Serve with fried rice or hot steamed rice.

5 to 6 servings

GINGERED SHERBET

1 pint lemon sherbet
2 tablespoons finely
   chopped, crystallized
   ginger
1 pint orange sherbet

Slightly soften lemon sherbet; stir in ginger. Refreeze. To serve, alternate scoops of lemon and orange sherbet in serving dishes. If desired, garnish with mint sprigs.

6 servings

These look like rolled cookies but are much easier to make.

ALMOND SUGAR COOKIES

1 cup sugar
1 cup powdered sugar
1 cup butter or
   margarine, softened
¾ cup plus 2 tablespoons
   cooking oil
2 eggs, well beaten
1 teaspoon vanilla
4 cups Pillsbury's Best
   All Purpose or
   Unbleached Flour
1 teaspoon soda
1 teaspoon cream of
   tartar
½ teaspoon salt
   Slivered almonds

Cream sugars and butter. Add oil, eggs and vanilla; mix. (Lightly spoon flour into measuring cup; level off.) Combine dry ingredients and stir into sugar mixture. Chill 2 hours. Preheat oven to 350°F. Shape dough into 1-inch balls. Place on ungreased cookie sheets. Flatten with glass dipped in sugar. Press slivered almond on each cookie. Bake 12 to 15 minutes until very light golden color.

9 to 10 dozen cookies

TIP: Baked cookies freeze well for future use.

HIGH ALTITUDE — above 3500 Feet: Reduce oil to ½ cup. Bake at 350°F. 12 to 15 minutes.

A little more effort? Yes. Difficult? No. This menu transports us to the informality of the French countryside where the fine foods of chateaus and wayside inns are recreated by chefs in the finest restaurants around the world. Treat your guests to an adventure in French dining, and don't be too timid to tackle the Escargot and Brioche if you haven't before. Directions are complete and easy to follow. Soup plates are perfect for serving the Bourguignonne so not a drop of the rich gravy will escape.

ESCARGOT

½ cup butter or
    margarine, softened
½ to 1 teaspoon garlic
    powder or instant
    minced garlic
1 tablespoon snipped
    parsley
    Dash nutmeg
4½-oz. can snails (about 24)
24 snail shells

Preheat oven to 400°F. Combine butter, garlic, parsley and nutmeg. Place 1 snail in each shell; top with about 1 teaspoon butter mixture. Bake, uncovered, 10 to 12 minutes or until snails are firm. Serve immediately with remaining butter sauce for dipping.

4 to 6 servings

Country French

Vichyssoise OR Escargot
Beef Bourguignonne
Caesar Salad
Speedy Brioche
Delicate Orange Crêpes

Serve well-chilled for a superb first course.

VICHYSSOISE

¼ cup chopped leeks or
    green onions
2 tablespoons chopped
    onions
2 tablespoons butter or
    margarine
2½ cups chicken broth
⅓ cup Hungry Jack®
    Mashed Potato Flakes
½ cup milk
1 cup light cream
1 teaspoon finely chopped
    chives

In saucepan, cook leeks and onions in butter until tender but not brown. Add broth and potato flakes. Cover and simmer 15 minutes. Puree in blender. Add milk and cream. Chill 2 to 3 hours to blend flavors and thicken. Serve with sprinkling of chopped chives.

6 (¾-cup) servings

BEEF BOURGUIGNONNE

2 tablespoons cooking oil
    or shortening
2 pounds sirloin steak, cut
    into 1½-inch cubes
1 medium green pepper,
    cut into 2-inch pieces
1 cup (8 oz.) sliced or
    quartered fresh
    mushrooms
2 tablespoons chopped
    onion or ½ teaspoon
    instant minced onion
2 tablespoons flour
1 teaspoon salt
⅔ cup dry red wine
1⅔ cups (16-oz. can)
    drained whole onions

Preheat oven to 400°F. Place oil in 2½-quart casserole. Add steak, green pepper, mushrooms and onion. Bake, uncovered, 30 minutes, stirring occasionally. Remove from oven; stir in flour and salt. Blend in wine and whole onions. Cover and bake 30 minutes longer. Serve over noodles or rice.

4 to 6 servings

Note that this salad should be served immediately after tossing.

CAESAR SALAD

- 1 clove garlic, cut in quarters
- ⅓ cup cooking oil
- ½ teaspoon salt
- ⅛ teaspoon pepper
- 2 quarts romaine lettuce
- 1 egg
- 2 tablespoons lemon juice
- ¼ cup grated Parmesan cheese
- 1 cup seasoned croutons
- 6 anchovy fillets, if desired

In small container, marinate garlic in oil 30 minutes; add salt and pepper. Tear romaine into bite-size pieces; place in salad bowl. Remove garlic pieces from oil; discard garlic. Pour oil over romaine; toss lightly. Break egg over salad; add lemon juice and toss again. Add cheese and croutons; toss. Garnish with anchovies. Serve immediately.

4 to 6 servings

SPEEDY BRIOCHE

- 2 pkg. active dry yeast
- ¼ cup warm water (105°-115°F.)
- 1¼ cups buttermilk or sour milk*
- ¾ cup butter or margarine, softened
- ⅓ cup sugar
- 3 teaspoons salt
- 2 teaspoons baking powder
- 2 eggs
- 5 to 5½ cups Pillsbury's Best All Purpose or Unbleached Flour

(Lightly spoon flour into measuring cup; level off.) Soften yeast in warm water in large bowl. Add buttermilk, butter, sugar, salt, baking powder, eggs and 2½ cups flour. Beat 2 minutes at medium speed. By hand, stir in remaining flour. On well-floured surface, knead dough until smooth and elastic, about 5 minutes. Grease (not oil) 24 brioche or medium muffin cups. Divide dough into 24 equal parts. Remove about ⅕ of dough from each. Shape all into smooth balls. Place larger balls in pans. With finger, make a deep indentation in center of large balls; place smaller balls in indentation. Cover; let rise in warm place until light and doubled in size, 30 to 45 minutes. Preheat oven to 350°F. Bake rolls 25 to 30 minutes until golden brown. Remove from pans and brush with butter. Serve warm.

2 dozen brioche

*To sour milk, use 1 tablespoon vinegar plus enough milk to make 1¼ cups.

HIGH ALTITUDE: No change.

Speedy Brioche

Delicate Orange Crêpes, p. 68

DELICATE ORANGE CRÊPES

½ cup (4 oz.) creamed
  cottage cheese
½ cup dairy sour cream
1½ teaspoons sugar
½ teaspoon salt
1½ teaspoons grated
  orange peel
1½ tablespoons orange
  juice
2 eggs
½ cup Pillsbury's Best All
  Purpose or Unbleached
  Flour
  Orange Honey Sauce
  (See below)
2 tablespoons brandy, if
  desired

In blender container or bowl, blend cottage cheese until fine. Add sour cream, sugar, salt, orange peel, juice, eggs and flour; blend at high speed until well-mixed. Heat a 6-inch crêpe pan* or fry pan over medium high heat. Grease lightly. Pour 3 tablespoons batter at a time, into pan, tilting to spread evenly over bottom. When crêpe is light brown and set, turn to brown other side. Roll warm crêpes; arrange in chafing dish or oblong serving dish. Pour hot Orange Honey Sauce over crêpes. To flame, warm brandy in small saucepan just until small bubbles form; ignite with match. Immediately pour over crêpes. If desired, serve with whipped cream.

5 to 6 servings

*A variety of crêpe pans are available; follow manufacturer's directions.

TIPS: Crêpes may be made in advance. Stack them between paper toweling; wrap and store in refrigerator or freezer.

For easy crêpes: Beat together 2 eggs, 1 cup milk, 3 tablespoons melted butter or margarine. Add ¾ cup Hungry Jack® Pancake Mix and beat until smooth. Prepare as directed above.

Orange Honey Sauce

½ cup honey
⅓ cup butter or
  margarine
¼ teaspoon cinnamon
2 teaspoons grated
  orange peel
2 tablespoons orange
  juice

Blend all ingredients in saucepan. Cook over medium heat, stirring occasionally, until hot. Serve over crêpes.

¾ cup sauce

German

Sauerbraten
Potato Dumplings
Buttered Carrots
Hot Cabbage Salad
Streamlined Apple Strudel

The German contributions to our repertoire of recipes are varied and memorable. This menu features just some of the specialties of the Bavarian culture which have become international favorites. Remember that the Sauerbraten must be marinated at least one day in advance of cooking, so purchase your meat early in preparation for this procedure. This is a bountiful feast, perfect for chilly weather and hearty eaters. Take your time at the table and savor each dish. Perhaps you might prefer to serve the Strudel and hot coffee about an hour after dinner when your guests are relaxing in the living or family room.

Streamlined Apple Strudel, p. 70

Choose the longer marinating time if you wish a stronger flavor. Gingersnaps add flavor and help thicken the traditional sauce.

SAUERBRATEN

- 3 to 3½-pound pot roast
- 1 cup red wine vinegar
- 1½ cups water
- 1 medium onion, sliced
- 1 stalk celery, sliced
- 5 whole cloves
- 2 bay leaves
- 3 teaspoons salt
- 4 peppercorns or ¼ teaspoon pepper
- 2 tablespoons cooking oil
- 2 tablespoons brown sugar
- 6 gingersnaps, crushed

Place meat in glass bowl. Add remaining ingredients except oil, brown sugar and gingersnaps. Cover and marinate in refrigerator 24 to 48 hours, turning meat several times to season evenly. Remove meat from marinade; drain well. In large fry pan or Dutch oven, brown meat on all sides in hot oil. Add 1½ cups strained marinade. Cover and simmer 2½ to 3 hours or until tender. Place meat on warm platter. Spoon fat off juice; add brown sugar and gingersnaps. Cook until mixture comes to a boil, stirring constantly. If necessary, thin with water or remaining marinade. Pour over meat. Serve with potato dumplings, boiled potatoes or potato pancakes.

6 to 8 servings

POTATO DUMPLINGS

- 1 quart water
- 1 teaspoon salt
- 6 medium potatoes, peeled, cooked and mashed (about 5 cups)
- 1½ cups Pillsbury's Best All Purpose Flour
- 2 eggs, slightly beaten
- 1 teaspoon baking powder
- 1 teaspoon salt

In saucepan, bring water and 1 teaspoon salt to boil. In bowl, combine remaining ingredients; mix until fluffy. Roll into 1-inch balls; drop into gently boiling water. Cook 5 to 7 minutes. Drain; serve warm.

36 dumplings

A new look for fresh carrots.

BUTTERED CARROTS

- ¼ cup butter or margarine
- 2 pounds small whole carrots, cooked and drained
- ¼ cup cognac
- ¼ cup firmly packed brown sugar
  Dash ground ginger

In medium saucepan, melt butter; add carrots and pour cognac over carrots. Sprinkle with sugar and ginger; cover. Cook slowly 10 minutes; uncover and continue cooking, stirring several times, for 10 minutes or until carrots are glazed.

6 to 8 servings

HOT CABBAGE SALAD

- ½ medium head cabbage, shredded
- 8 strips bacon
  Cider vinegar
- 2 tablespoons sugar
- ½ teaspoon salt

Place cabbage in bowl. Fry bacon until crisp; crumble over cabbage. In same fry pan, combine drippings and an equal amount of vinegar; add sugar and salt. Heat to boiling; pour over cabbage. Toss lightly. Serve warm.

6 to 8 servings

STREAMLINED APPLE STRUDEL

- 8-oz. can Pillsbury Refrigerated Quick Crescent Dinner Rolls
- ¼ cup butter or margarine
- ½ cup dry bread crumbs
- 2 tablespoons sugar
- 4 cups (4 medium) unpeeled, shredded apples, drained
- ½ cup sugar
- 1 to 2 tablespoons lemon juice
- 1 teaspoon cinnamon
- 1 teaspoon vanilla
  Powdered sugar

Separate crescent dough into 2 rectangles. On lightly-floured pastry cloth, place dough rectangles together, overlapping edges to form a 13x7-inch rectangle. Firmly press edges and perforations to seal. Roll out dough to about 16x14-inch rectangle. Let dry while preparing crumbs and filling. Melt butter; stir in crumbs. Cool. Sprinkle evenly over dough to within ½ inch of edge. Sprinkle with 2 tablespoons sugar. Preheat oven to 350°F. Combine apples with ½ cup sugar, lemon juice, cinnamon and vanilla. Starting with one 14-inch side of rectangle, spread apple filling over ⅓ of dough to within 1 inch of edge. Starting with apple side, roll up jelly-roll fashion. Place diagonally, seam-side down, on ungreased 15x10-inch jelly roll pan. Tuck ends under. Using a sharp knife, cut slits across top about 2 inches apart. Bake 35 to 40 minutes or until golden brown. Cut in half; carefully remove from pan immediately. Sprinkle with powdered sugar. Cut into slices; serve warm.

6 to 8 servings

TIP: If desired, add ½ cup raisins or currants to filling.

HIGH ALTITUDE: No change.

Italian

Antipasto Platter
Garlic Rounds
Chicken Cacciatore
Fettuccini al Burro
Orange-Lemon Ice

Aromatic cheeses, glistening marinades, pinches of pungent herbs and rich tomato sauces — some of the gastronomic joys of "eating Italian." This menu combines these inviting Old World flavors into a company meal that lends itself to either the elegant or the casual dinner party approach. You will want to borrow the Antipasto Platter to use for other occasions, too; the combinations are versatile and the "spread" can be as light or hearty as you desire. Only the Garlic Rounds and the Fettuccini require last minute attention, so you need not leave the party for long.

ANTIPASTO TRAY

An antipasto tray can serve as a salad, main dish or appetizer, depending upon the amounts and kinds of vegetables and meats that are included. Usually the vegetables are marinated or chilled for about 8 hours before serving.

Vegetables can include: asparagus spears, cauliflowerettes, sliced cucumber, beets, olives, mushroom caps, artichoke hearts and/or cherry tomatoes. Marinate vegetables in a dressing such as Italian, oil and vinegar, or French. Drain and arrange artfully in separate sections on tray or platter.

Other foods to add: sliced salami or luncheon meats; sliced and chilled, cooked roast or ham; hard-cooked or deviled eggs; sliced cheeses; chilled, canned salmon; shrimp, crabmeat or tuna and/or pickles or peppers.

Adjust the amount of garlic powder to suit your own taste.

GARLIC ROUNDS

    8-oz. can Pillsbury Refrigerated Buttermilk or Country Style Biscuits
    ¼ cup butter or margarine, softened
    ⅛ to ¼ teaspoon garlic powder
    Grated Parmesan cheese
    Paprika

Bake biscuits as directed on package. Split each biscuit in half. Combine softened butter and garlic powder; spread over biscuits. Sprinkle with cheese and paprika. Place on ungreased cookie sheet. Broil until lightly browned. Serve warm.

20 pieces

HIGH ALTITUDE: No change.

If desired, ¼ cup of dry red wine or dry sherry may be added to the sauce.

CHICKEN CACCIATORE
  2½ to 3-pound frying
     chicken, cut up
  3 tablespoons cooking oil
     or olive oil
 15-oz. can tomato sauce
  6-oz. can tomato paste
  1 medium onion, sliced
     or chopped
  1 teaspoon salt
  1 teaspoon Italian
     seasoning or leaf
     oregano
  2 gloves garlic, minced
  ⅛ teaspoon pepper

In large fry pan or Dutch oven, brown chicken in hot oil. Drain excess oil. Stir in remaining ingredients. Reduce heat, cover and simmer 45 to 50 minutes until tender. Serve over Fettuccini al Burro or spaghetti.

4 to 6 servings

For variety in taste and color, use green noodles in place of plain.

FETTUCCINI AL BURRO
 10-oz. pkg. egg noodles
  ¼ cup butter or
     margarine, melted
  ½ cup grated Parmesan
     cheese

Cook noodles as directed on package. Drain. Add butter and cheese; toss to coat noodles.

5 to 6 (1 cup) servings

Delightfully refreshing – the perfect ending for a rich meal.

ORANGE-LEMON ICE
  2 cups water
  1 cup sugar
  1 cup orange juice
  ¼ cup lemon juice
  1 tablespoon grated
     orange peel
  1 tablespoon grated
     lemon peel

In saucepan, bring water and sugar to boil; boil 5 minutes. Cool to room temperature; add juices and peels. Pour into 8-inch square pan. Freeze 3 to 4 hours, stirring every ½ hour. (Volume increases as it is stirred.)

6 (1 cup) servings

English Classic
Standing Beef Rib Roast
Yorkshire Pudding
Brussels Sprouts Royale
Spicy Chilled Fruit Salad
Easy Cheesy Apple Pie

A menu fit for a king. Or, more practically, when the boss is coming to dinner, for a Dickensonian Christmas feast or anytime a deluxe dinner is in order. No casual buffet, but rather an elegant sit-down affair which you will find to be surprisingly uncomplicated. The salad and dessert are handsome make-aheads, and except for the carving of the roast, only the Yorkshire Pudding and the vegetable will give the hostess last minute kitchen duty. Note our suggestions for easy carving so your roast will look as good as it tastes.

Yorkshire Pudding
Brussels Sprouts Royale
Standing Beef Rib Roast

A horseradish sauce makes a zesty accompaniment for this magnificent roast.

STANDING BEEF RIB ROAST

Standing rib roast
Salt
Pepper

Season roast with salt and pepper. Place roast, fat side up, in open shallow roasting pan. Insert meat thermometer so the bulb reaches the center of the largest muscle, being sure that the bulb does not rest in fat or on bone. (Do not add water; do not cover.) Roast at 325°F. to desired degree of doneness. Allow about 1 to 2 servings per pound.

How to Carve

Place the roast on the platter with the largest end down to form a solid base. Insert the fork between the two top ribs. Starting on the fat side, carve across the grain to the rib bone. Use the tip of the knife to cut along the rib bone to loosen the slice. Be sure to keep close to the bone, to make the largest servings possible. Slide the knife back under the slice and, steadying it with the fork, lift the slice to the side of the platter. If the platter is not large enough, place the slices on a heated platter close by.

A delicious alternative to potatoes or rice. The English bake a popover batter in drippings from roast beef. The batter first puffs up, then collapses in the center. Serve cut into squares with meat juices or gravy.

YORKSHIRE PUDDING

2 tablespoons roast beef drippings
2 eggs
1 cup Pillsbury's Best All Purpose or Unbleached Flour
1 cup milk
½ teaspoon salt

Preheat oven to 425°F. Pour drippings into 9-inch square or round pan; tilt pan to grease sides. In mixing bowl, beat eggs slightly. (Lightly spoon flour into measuring cup; level off.) Add remaining ingredients and beat just until smooth. Do not overbeat. Pour batter into pan. Bake 15 minutes, then reduce temperature to 350°F. Bake 10 to 15 minutes longer until golden brown.

6 servings

Timetable for Roasting

Weight	Doneness	Meat Thermometer Reading	Approximate Cooking Time Per Pound
4 to 6 lbs.	Rare	140°F.	26 to 32 min.
	Medium	160°F.	34 to 38 min.
	Well	170°F.	40 to 42 min.
6 to 8 lbs.	Rare	140°F.	23 to 25 min.
	Medium	160°F.	27 to 30 min.
	Well	170°F.	32 to 35 min.

BRUSSELS SPROUTS ROYALE

- 2 pkg. (10 oz. each) brussels sprouts frozen in butter sauce
- 1 cup seedless green grapes
- 3 tablespoons sauterne
- 1 to 2 tablespoons slivered almonds

Cook brussels sprouts as directed on package. Partially open pouch; drain butter sauce into small saucepan. Add grapes. Cook only enough to heat through. Remove from heat; add sauterne and slivered almonds. Toss with brussels sprouts.

6 servings

Start this one early so it has time to chill thoroughly before serving. Delicious with both poultry and with game.

SPICY CHILLED FRUIT SALAD

- 3½ cups (two 16-oz. cans) drained fruits for salad (reserve syrup)
- 1 cup sugar
- 1½ cups liquid (fruit syrup plus water)
- ½ cup vinegar
- 10 whole cloves
- 1 to 2 sticks cinnamon Lettuce

In medium saucepan, combine sugar, liquid, vinegar, cloves and cinnamon; simmer, uncovered, 10 minutes. Add fruits; bring to boil. Cover and cool. Refrigerate until thoroughly chilled, at least 2 hours. Remove cloves and cinnamon sticks. Drain; arrange on lettuce leaves.

6 servings

Nothing at all to making this crust; it is quickly accomplished right in the pie pan.

EASY CHEESY APPLE PIE

- 1 cup Pillsbury's Best All Purpose or Unbleached Flour
- ¼ cup quick-cooking rolled oats
- 1½ teaspoons sugar
- ½ teaspoon salt
- ⅓ cup cooking oil
- ¼ cup cold milk
- 1 pkg. (4-serving size) vanilla pudding and pie filling mix (not instant)
- 5½ to 6 cups (6 medium) peeled, sliced cooking apples
- ½ cup (2 oz.) shredded Cheddar cheese

Topping

- ⅓ cup flour
- ⅓ cup sugar
- ¼ cup quick-cooking rolled oats
- 3 tablespoons butter or margarine, softened

Preheat oven to 375°F. (Lightly spoon flour into measuring cup; level off.) In 9-inch pie pan, combine first six ingredients; mix well. Press onto bottom and sides of pie pan; do not press onto rim. In large bowl, combine dry pudding mix and apples; spoon into unbaked crust. Sprinkle with cheese. Combine Topping ingredients; blend until crumbly. Sprinkle over cheese. Bake 45 to 50 minutes until light golden brown and apples are tender. Serve warm.

9-inch pie

HIGH ALTITUDE — above 3500 Feet: Bake at 375°F. 55 to 60 minutes.

Larger Gatherings

Don't be intimidated by cooking for a few more than usual — if you can do it for six, you can do it for twelve. Of course, you will need more food, and maybe you'll decide to keep the menu and the style of serving a little less elaborate. But with a little forethought and an assist from this chapter, you can approach the big day with confident anticipation. If you don't have room to seat everyone at tables, don't worry. Just choose a menu that can be eaten easily with a fork (nothing to cut and little to spill) and supply enough chairs so everyone has a comfortable place to park with their plate. As a rule, guests don't mind being a bit crowded. In fact, the informality and the unavoidable "mixing" are often super stimuli to lively conversation that includes even the shy violet in the group.

Invite your neighbors or other friends in for a unique midmorning coffee break and surprise them with a smorgasbord of international brews and a handsome array of homemade breads. Something for everyone — sweet coffee cake, a golden, fruit-laden loaf, piping hot scones and moist bran muffins. And to top them all, delectable whipped butters. Brew the usual amount of coffee for the number of guests being entertained and provide them with the instructions, ingredients and utensils to mix their own foreign favorites.

P.S. Better have your bread recipes on hand, too, because they are sure to be requested.

A Italian Coffee
B Arabian Coffee
C Swedish Coffee
D Brazilian Coffee
E Blonde Date Nut Bread
F Mexican Coffee
G Scotch Scones
H Whipped Butter
I Maple Nut Coffee Twist
J Bran Muffins

Coffee Party Extraordinaire

International Brews
Maple-Nut Coffee Twist
Blonde Date-Nut Bread
Scotch Scones
Bran Muffins
Whipped Butters

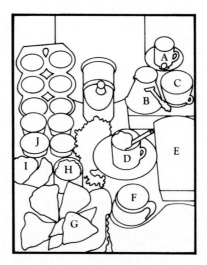

INTERNATIONAL BREWS

SWEDISH

¼ cup brown sugar
¼ teaspoon cinnamon
¼ teaspoon ground cloves
¼ teaspoon nutmeg
Orange peel
Strong hot coffee
Whipped cream or topping

Combine first four ingredients; mix well. Place 1 teaspoon spice mixture in each serving cup. Add strip of orange peel. Fill cup with coffee; stir. Top with whipped cream.

MEXICAN

Place 2 teaspoons chocolate syrup and ⅛ teaspoon cinnamon in each serving cup. Fill cup with strong hot coffee; stir well. Top with whipped cream or topping; sprinkle with cinnamon and nutmeg.

BRAZILIAN

Place 2 tablespoons instant cocoa mix in each serving cup. Fill cup with strong hot coffee. Stir with cinnamon stick. Top with whipped cream or topping.

TURKISH

Place 1 tablespoon honey or sugar and 1 crushed cardamom seed in each serving cup. Fill cup with strong hot coffee; stir. Top with whipped cream or topping.

VIENNESE

Fill each serving cup with strong hot coffee. Stir in 1 teaspoon sugar. Top with whipped cream or topping; sprinkle with nutmeg.

ARABIAN

Place 1 crushed cardamom seed in each serving cup. Fill cup with strong hot coffee. Stir with cinnamon stick.

ITALIAN

Fill each serving cup with strong hot coffee. Serve with a twist of lemon.

FRENCH

To prepare café au lait, two pots are needed — one for strong hot coffee and one for an equal amount of hot milk or cream. Pour from both pots at the same time into each serving cup.

MAPLE-NUT COFFEE TWIST

   ¾ cup milk
   ¼ cup butter or margarine
   2¾ to 3 cups Pillsbury's Best All Purpose or Unbleached Flour
   3 tablespoons sugar
   ½ teaspoon salt
   1 pkg. active dry yeast
   1 teaspoon maple flavoring
   1 egg
   ¼ cup butter or margarine, melted

Filling

   ½ cup sugar
   ⅓ cup chopped nuts
   1 teaspoon cinnamon
   1 teaspoon maple flavoring

Glaze

   1 cup powdered sugar
   2 tablespoons butter or margarine, melted
   1 to 2 tablespoons milk or water
   ½ teaspoon maple flavoring

In small saucepan, heat milk and butter until very warm (120° to 130° F.). (Lightly spoon flour into measuring cup; level off.) In large bowl, combine warm liquid, 1 cup flour, sugar, salt, yeast, flavoring and egg; beat 2 minutes at medium speed. By hand, stir in remaining flour to make a soft dough. On floured surface, knead dough until smooth and elastic, about 2 minutes. Place in greased bowl. Cover; let rise in warm place until light and doubled in size, 45 to 60 minutes. In small bowl, combine Filling ingredients; set aside. Grease 12-inch pizza pan. Punch down dough; divide and shape into three balls. Roll out or press one ball of dough to cover bottom of greased pizza pan. Brush dough with about ⅓ of melted butter; sprinkle with ⅓ of Filling. Repeat layers of dough, melted butter and Filling. To shape, place a glass about 2-inches in diameter in center of dough. With scissors, cut from outside edge to the glass, forming 16 pie-shaped wedges. Twist each wedge five times. Remove glass. Let rise until doubled in size, 30 to 45 minutes. Preheat oven to 375° F. Bake 18 to 22 minutes until golden brown. Cool 5 minutes; remove from pan. In small bowl, blend Glaze ingredients until smooth. Drizzle over warm coffee cake.

One 12-inch coffee cake

HIGH ALTITUDE: No change.

A great plus is that you can make up some batter for today and store the remainder in your refrigerator to go with next week's coffee.

BRAN MUFFINS

   3 cups whole-bran wheat cereal
   1 cup boiling water
   ½ cup solid shortening or cooking oil
   2 eggs
   2½ cups Pillsbury's Best All Purpose or Unbleached Flour
   1½ cups sugar
   2½ teaspoons soda
   2 cups buttermilk or sour milk*

Preheat oven to 400° F. In large bowl, combine cereal and boiling water. Stir in shortening and eggs. (Lightly spoon flour into measuring cup; level off.) Add remaining ingredients; blend well. Spoon batter into desired number of greased (not oiled) muffin cups or muffin cups lined with paper baking cups, filling ¾ full. (Remaining batter may be stored up to 6 weeks in tightly covered container in refrigerator.) Bake 18 to 22 minutes until golden brown.

2 to 2½ dozen muffins

*To sour milk, use 2 tablespoons vinegar plus enough milk to make 2 cups.

TIP: One cup chopped dates, raisins or chopped nuts may be added to batter.

HIGH ALTITUDE — Above 3500 Feet: Bake at 400° F. for 20 to 25 minutes.

SCOTCH SCONES

- 2 cups Pillsbury's Best All Purpose or Unbleached Flour
- 2 tablespoons sugar
- 3 teaspoons baking powder
- 1 teaspoon salt
- ¼ teaspoon soda
- ½ cup raisins or currants, if desired
- ¼ cup cooking oil
- ½ cup dairy sour cream
- 3 tablespoons milk
- 1 egg, slightly beaten

Preheat oven to 425° F. (Lightly spoon flour into measuring cup; level off.) In bowl, combine first six ingredients. Add remaining ingredients, stirring until dough clings together. On floured surface, toss dough to lightly coat with flour. Knead 12 to 15 times. Divide dough in half. Pat each ball of dough to a 6-inch circle with top slightly rounded. Brush surface with milk; sprinkle with sugar. Cut each circle into 6 wedges. Place 2 inches apart on cookie sheet. Bake 10 to 12 minutes until golden brown. Serve hot with butter and honey, or raspberry or strawberry jam.

1 dozen scones

HIGH ALTITUDE: above 3500 Feet: Reduce baking powder to 2 teaspoons.
Bake at 450° F. 10 to 12 minutes.

WHIPPED BUTTER

In small bowl, cream ½ cup butter until soft. Slowly beat in 2 tablespoons milk or cream. Beat on highest speed until light and fluffy.

1 cup

Variations:

Honey Butter — Omit milk; gradually add ¼ cup honey, beating until light.

Marmalade Butter — Omit milk; gradually add ¼ cup marmalade, beating until light.

Maple Butter — Substitute maple-flavored syrup for milk.

Orange Butter — Substitute orange juice for milk and add 1 tablespoon grated orange peel.

BLONDE DATE-NUT BREAD

- ⅓ cup butter or margarine, softened
- ¾ cup sugar
- 2 eggs
- ¾ cup buttermilk or sour milk*
- 2 cups Pillsbury's Best All Purpose or Unbleached Flour
- ½ teaspoon soda
- ½ teaspoon baking powder
- ½ teaspoon salt
- 1 cup chopped dates
- ½ cup chopped nuts

Preheat oven to 350° F. Grease (not oil) bottom only of 9x5-inch loaf pan. In bowl, cream butter and sugar. Beat in eggs; blend in buttermilk. Stir in remaining ingredients just until blended. Pour into greased pan. Bake 50 to 55 minutes until toothpick inserted in center comes out clean.

1 loaf

*To sour milk, use 1 tablespoon vinegar plus enough milk to make ¾ cup.

HIGH ALTITUDE — Above 3500 Feet: Bake at 375° F. for 50 to 55 minutes.

So often at birthday parties, children "feast" on candy, ice cream and other goodies only to come home unable to eat a nourishing dinner. Since it costs relatively little to serve a nourishing, kid-pleasing lunch or supper, why not try it at your child's next party? Finger food is the main attraction here with a fork needed only for the gelatin and Clown Cake. All their special favorites are included, and they won't even notice the vitamins tucked inside!

CHEESE 'N WIENER CRESCENTS

    8 wieners
    8 strips Cheddar
        cheese
    8-oz. can Pillsbury
        Refrigerated Quick
        Crescent Dinner Rolls

Preheat oven to 375°F. Slit wieners to within ½ inch of ends; insert cheese strips. Separate crescent dough into 8 triangles. Place a wiener on wide end of each triangle; roll up. Place on ungreased cookie sheet, cheese-side-up. Bake 10 to 15 minutes until golden brown.

8 sandwiches

To reheat, wrap in foil; heat at 350°F. for 10 to 15 minutes.

HIGH ALTITUDE: No change.

VEGETABLE TEASERS

Carrot Curls: Slice carrots lengthwise with vegetable peeler; roll up and secure with toothpick. Chill in ice water.

Peanut Butter-stuffed Celery: Cut celery stalks into 2-inch pieces. Fill with peanut butter.

Happy Birthday Party
Cheese and Wiener Crescents
Gelatin Cubes
Vegetable Teasers
Party Time Cake Cones
OR
Clown Cake

Rutabaga Flowers or Stars: Slice rutabaga into thin slices. Cut with small scalloped or star-shaped cookie or canape cutters.

CLOWN CAKE

Grease (not oil) and flour two 8-inch round layer pans and one 5-oz. custard cup. Prepare your favorite Pillsbury Plus Cake Mix as directed on package. Spread batter in prepared pans. Bake layers as directed; bake cupcake 15 to 20 minutes. Remove from pans and cool. Frost layers as for a 2-layer cake. Place cupcake on top for a "hat;" frost. Decorate cake as a clown face with small candies and decorator icing.

2-layer cake

PARTY TIME CAKE CONES

Prepare and bake your favorite flavor cupcakes as directed on Pillsbury Plus Cake Mix package. When cool, insert small end of cupcakes into cup-type ice cream cones. Prepare your favorite frosting; frost cupcakes. Decorate as desired to resemble animals, clowns or sundaes.

24 to 30 cupcakes.

Satisfy those robust teen appetites and appeal to their preference for the casual with this Italian-flavored menu. They'll be standing three deep to heap their plates with our spicy Lasagna recipe and the crisp tossed salad. Keep it simple with just a plate, fork and napkin. It's more comfortable for them and certainly easier for you. And what a rousing success the Sundae Bar will be. Have several flavors of ice cream along with the toppings, spoons and dishes arranged buffet fashion. Let the guests "build" their own creation or have a few "soda jerks" on hand to help with the serving. Why not freeze the ice cream balls in advance? Just scoop the balls onto a waxed paper-lined pan and freeze until firm. You're sure to be on the hostess hit parade after this smashing success!

Teen Time
Lasagna
Hot Garlic Bread
Tossed Salad
with your choice of dressing
Sundae Bar

A make-ahead, bake later speciality that will become one of your most cherished recipes.

LASAGNA

    1 pound ground beef
    ¼ cup chopped onion or 1
        tablespoon instant minced
        onion

1½ cups water
   8-oz. can tomato sauce
   6-oz. can tomato paste
   4-oz. can mushroom stems
      and pieces, drained
   1 clove garlic, crushed or ⅛
      teaspoon garlic powder
   1 teaspoon leaf basil
   1 teaspoon snipped parsley or
      ½ teaspoon parsley flakes
   1 teaspoon salt
   ½ teaspoon leaf oregano
   ¼ teaspoon pepper
   8 oz. lasagna noodles
   2 cups creamed cottage cheese
   1 cup chopped fresh spinach, if
      desired
   2 tablespoons diced salami, if
      desired
   1 egg
   1 cup (4 oz.) shredded
      Mozzarella cheese
   ¼ cup grated Parmesan cheese

In large fry pan, brown ground beef
and onion; drain. Add water,
tomato sauce and paste,
mushrooms, garlic, basil, parsley, ½
teaspoon salt, oregano and ⅛
teaspoon pepper; simmer 1 hour
over low heat, stirring occasionally.
Cook lasagna noodles as directed
on package. In large bowl,
combine cottage cheese, spinach,
salami, egg, ½ teaspoon salt and ¼
teaspoon pepper; mix well. In
13x9-inch pan, layer 2 thicknesses
of noodles, ½ cottage cheese
mixture, ½ meat mixture and ½
Mozzarella cheese; repeat layers
using 1 layer of noodles. Sprinkle
with Parmesan cheese. Bake at
350° F. for 30 minutes. Remove

from oven; let stand 15 minutes for
ease in cutting.

6 to 8 servings

TIP: May be assembled up to 24
hours ahead. Cover and refrigerate.
Bake about 40 minutes.

HOT GARLIC BREAD

   16 to 20-inch loaf French bread
   ½ cup butter or margarine,
      softened
   ½ teaspoon garlic salt

Preheat oven to 350° F. Cut French
bread diagonally into 1-inch slices.
Combine butter and garlic salt; mix
well. Spread on slices; reassemble
loaf. Wrap in foil; heat 15 minutes.
Serve hot.

6 to 8 servings

SUNDAE BAR

PINEAPPLE WHIPPED CREAM

   ½ cup whipping cream
   2 tablespoons powdered sugar
   ¼ cup well-drained, crushed
      pineapple
   1½ teaspoons lemon juice
   ½ teaspoon vanilla

Beat cream until stiff. Combine
remaining ingredients; fold into
whipped cream.

1 cup

COCONUT WHIPPED CREAM

   ½ cup flaked coconut
   2 tablespoons sugar
   1 teaspoon grated orange peel
   1 tablespoon orange
      juice
   1½ teaspoons lemon juice
   ½ teaspoon vanilla
   ½ cup whipping cream

Combine first six ingredients; chill
15 minutes. In bowl, beat cream
until stiff. Fold coconut mixture
into whipped cream.

1½ cups

HOT CARAMEL SUNDAE SAUCE

   1½ cups sugar
   ½ cup light corn syrup
   6 tablespoons butter
   1 cup light cream
   ½ teaspoon salt
   ½ teaspoon vanilla

In saucepan, combine sugar, corn
syrup, 3 tablespoons butter and ½
cup cream. Bring to boil; gradually
add remaining cream and butter.
Cook over medium heat, stirring
occasionally, to soft ball stage
(230° F.). Remove from heat; add
salt and vanilla. Serve warm.

2 cups

HOT FUDGE SUNDAE SAUCE

   1 cup sugar
   2 tablespoons flour
   ½ teaspoon salt
   1 cup water
   2 squares (2 oz.) unsweetened
      chocolate
   2 tablespoons butter
   1 teaspoon vanilla

In saucepan, combine sugar, flour
and salt; blend in water. Add
chocolate. Cook over medium
heat, stirring constantly, until
mixture comes to a full boil. Boil 1
minute. Remove from heat. Blend
in butter and vanilla. Serve hot.

1½ cups

BUTTERSCOTCH SUNDAE SAUCE

1½ cups firmly packed brown sugar
½ cup light corn syrup
⅓ cup butter or margarine
⅔ cup light cream

In saucepan, combine brown sugar, corn syrup and butter. Cook over medium heat, stirring occasionally, to soft ball stage (234° F.). Cool 5 minutes. Blend in cream. Serve hot or cold.

2 cups

STRAWBERRY SUNDAE SAUCE

10-oz. pkg. frozen strawberries, thawed
2 teaspoons cornstarch
2 to 3 drops red food coloring, if desired

Drain strawberries; reserve syrup. In saucepan, combine strawberry syrup and cornstarch. Cook over medium heat, stirring constantly until mixture is thick; boil 1 minute. Remove from heat. Add strawberries and food coloring. Cool before serving.

1 cup

Family Reunion

Golden Oven-Fried Chicken
Confetti Vegetable Salad
Party Potato Salad
Graham Snacker Buns
Strawberry Puff Ring

When everyone gets together, from the oldsters to the toddlers, your best friend is a menu which appeals to all ages, has make-ahead advantages and is simple to eat and serve. Well, — here it is. Some of the recipes are back by popular demand, and others offer a new twist — all sure-fire compliment catchers! To help you feel like a guest yourself, we've included two do-ahead salads and a golden oven-fried chicken which requires no messy stove-top browning. It's a bountiful spread with a very happy ending...sure to help make the day one for the memory book.

A different version of the three-bean salad.

CONFETTI VEGETABLE SALAD

16-oz. can cut green beans, drained
12-oz. can whole kernel corn, drained
17-oz. can peas, drained
2 jars (4½ oz. each) sliced mushrooms, drained
1 large onion, thinly sliced and separated into rings
¼ cup diced pimento

Dressing
⅔ cup cooking oil
⅔ cup wine vinegar
⅓ cup sugar
2 teaspoons salt

Combine first six ingredients in large bowl. Combine Dressing ingredients in container with tight cover. Cover; shake well. Pour dressing over bean mixture; toss to combine. Cover; refrigerate several hours or overnight.

12 (¾ cup) servings

TIP: Salad keeps a week in the refrigerator.

Almonds and Parmesan cheese make the coating super special.

GOLDEN OVEN-FRIED CHICKEN

1½ cups (¾ pound) butter or margarine
2 gloves garlic, crushed or minced
2 cups dry bread crumbs
½ cup grated Parmesan cheese
½ cup finely chopped almonds
4 tablespoons snipped parsley
2 teaspoons salt
½ teaspoon ground thyme or poultry seasoning
¼ teaspoon pepper
3 frying chickens (2½ to 3 pounds each), cut up or quartered

In two 13x9-inch pans, melt butter with garlic. In bowl or shallow pan, combine bread crumbs, cheese, almonds, parsley, salt, thyme and pepper; mix well. Dip chicken pieces in garlic butter and then in crumb mixture. Place skin-side-up in baking pan containing garlic butter. Bake at 400° F., uncovered, about 1 hour until tender, basting occasionally with pan drippings.

12 servings

Strawberry Puff Ring, p. 64

Graham crackers add the delicious flavor and currants or raisins spark these tender buns.

GRAHAM SNACKER BUNS

12 squares graham crackers or ⅔ cup graham cracker crumbs
½ cup currants or raisins
1 cup very warm water (120°-130° F.)
1 pkg. Pillsbury Hot Roll Mix
1 egg
¼ cup butter or margarine, melted

In large bowl, combine first three ingredients until crackers soften. Add yeast from hot roll mix; stir to dissolve. Stir in egg. Add flour mixture; blend well. Cover; let rise in warm place until light and doubled in size, 45 to 60 minutes. Grease (not oil) 16 muffin cups or 13x9-inch pan. On floured surface, toss dough until no longer sticky. Divide dough into 16 pieces; shape into balls. Place in muffin cups or pan; brush tops with half of butter. Let rise in warm place until light and doubled in size, 30 to 45 minutes. Preheat oven to 375° F. Bake 20 to 25 minutes until golden brown. Remove from pan. Brush tops with remaining butter.

16 rolls

HIGH ALTITUDE — Above 3500 Feet: Bake at 400° F. for 20 to 25 minutes.

PARTY POTATO SALAD

6 to 8 medium potatoes, cooked, peeled and sliced
½ cup French dressing
½ cup (1 medium) chopped onion or green onions
½ cup chopped pickle or pickle relish
2 teaspoons salt
⅛ teaspoon pepper
6 hard-cooked eggs, chopped
4 stalks celery, chopped
1 cup mayonnaise or salad dressing

Toss warm potato slices with French dressing, onion, pickles, salt and pepper. Cover and refrigerate overnight. Just before serving, mix in egg, celery and mayonnaise.

12 (¾ cup) servings

STRAWBERRY PUFF RING

6 tablespoons butter or margarine
¾ cup hot water
¾ cup Pillsbury's Best All Purpose or Unbleached Flour
½ teaspoon salt
3 eggs
2 pints (4 cups) fresh strawberries, sliced and chilled

Cream Filling
1 pkg. (6-serving size) vanilla pudding and pie filling mix
3 cups milk

Glaze
1 cup powdered sugar
2 to 3 tablespoons warm water
Almond flavoring, if desired

Preheat oven to 425° F. (Lightly spoon flour into measuring cup; level off.) In saucepan, combine butter and water; bring to a boil. Add flour and salt all at once; cook over medium heat, stirring constantly until mixture leaves sides of pan in smooth, compact ball, about 2 minutes. Cool 1 minute. Add eggs, one at a time, beating vigorously after each until mixture is smooth and glossy. Spoon 12 mounds of dough, just touching, in ring shape, about 8 inches in diameter on greased (not oiled) cookie sheet. Bake 30 to 35 minutes until golden brown. Turn off oven. Prick puff with sharp knife; leave in oven 20 minutes to dry out center. Cool. Prepare pudding mix with milk as directed on package. Cover and cool. Chill completely, 1 or 2 hours. In small mixing bowl combine Glaze ingredients; mix until smooth. Slice off top of puff. Spoon Cream Filling into bottom. Top with fresh berries. Replace top and drizzle with Glaze; garnish with strawberries, if desired.

12 servings

TIP: Puff may be filled and refrigerated 3 to 4 hours before serving. Best if served the day it is assembled. Puff may be baked a day ahead.

HIGH ALTITUDE: No change.

Cocktail Party

A CROWD FOR COCKTAILS

One of the few occasions where people don't mind being elbow-to-elbow for a few hours is at a stimulating cocktail party where the guest list is selective (in other words, you didn't invite everyone in town whom you "owe"), the conversation is lively and the spread, sumptuous. Especially if your dining area is a bit limited for sit-down dinners, why not pull out all the stops and serve up a sensational cocktail party? A few important "Do's" to remember. Have an ample supply of ice, glasses and cocktail fixings. Arrange the bar away from the food to avoid traffic jams. If the guest list is long and your budget can handle it, hire an experienced bartender; otherwise, allow plenty of room for guests to mix their own drinks. Have non-alcoholic beverages readily available. Strive for a balance of hot and cold foods, some that can be passed and others which can be placed strategically throughout the room. Plan your liquor purchasing carefully (with the help of our handy guide) so you are not sneaking out the back door to the store to augment a dwindling supply. And do make an effort to enliven the party by introducing guests and encouraging them to mingle with strangers as well as old friends. Another word to the wise: have some coffee perking for that "one for the road"—an important extra that will build your reputation as a thoughtful, considerate hostess.

HOW MUCH LIQUOR SHOULD YOU BUY?

Scotch, Bourbon, blended whiskey, gin, rum and vodka are the basic bar liquors.

For liquor, allow about 17 drinks (1½ oz. each) from a fifth of liquor (⁴/₅ qt.), or about 21 drinks from a quart. If you're entertaining a few couples and you know that a particular kind is enjoyed by some, purchase a small bottle. For larger groups, it's usually more economical to buy quarts. Keep drink garnishes such as onions, olives, cherries, lemons, oranges, etc., handy. Have a variety of mixes—both sweet and sour.

If serving wine straight from the bottle, allow around 8 to 10 drinks from a ⁴/₅-quart bottle. For a refreshing summer drink, serve wine mixed with a carbonated beverage such as lemon-lime. This is a good way to "stretch" wine.

Check with your local retailer for more information and recipes.

Number of People You're Having	For Pre-Dinner Cocktails You'll Average (2-3 drinks per person)	For a Party You'll Average (3-4 drinks per person)
4	8-12 drinks (⁴/₅ qt. req.)	12-16 drinks (⁴/₅ qt. req.)
6	12-18 drinks (Two ⁴/₅ qts. req.)	18-24 drinks (Two ⁴/₅ qts. req.)
8	16-24 drinks (Two ⁴/₅ qts. req.)	24-32 drinks (Two ⁴/₅ qts. req.)
12	24-36 drinks (Three ⁴/₅ qts. req.)	36-48 drinks (Three ⁴/₅ qts. req.)
20	40-60 drinks (4 qts. req.)	60-80 drinks (4 qts. req.)
40	80-120 drinks (6 qts. req.)	120-160 drinks (8 qts. req.)

COCKTAIL NUTS

2 tablespoons butter or margarine
¼ teaspoon seasoned salt
Dash Tabasco sauce
¼ teaspoon garlic powder
3 to 4 cups (1 pound) mixed nuts
3 tablespoons Worcestershire sauce

Melt butter with seasoned salt, Tabasco and garlic powder in shallow baking pan. Add nuts, tossing to coat. Bake at 300°F. for 15 minutes, stirring occasionally. Sprinkle with Worcestershire sauce and continue baking 15 minutes or until crisp.

3 to 4 cups

BASIC PREPARATION OF APPETIZERS

Many appetizers can be made ahead, some partially, others completely. A few appetizers, such as dips, are often better when made ahead so flavors have time to blend. Just remember to bring refrigerated dips to room temperature before serving (unless, of course, they are to be served hot).

Guests or hostess can cook their own broiled hors d'oeuvres on hibachis or grills.

When serving appetizers hot, use a warming device that has controllable warm heat such as a chafing dish, electric fondue pot, fry pan, warming tray or a flameproof container over a candle warmer.

FINGER FOODS-ON-A-PICK

These appetizers are conveniently served on toothpicks or bamboo skewers. Colored picks are pretty, and any combination of the following foods can be attractively arranged as a "pincushion" centerpiece using a pineapple half (cut lengthwise), an apple, grapefruit or orange half, eggplant, cabbage or an endive-covered styrofoam "tree."

Cheese cubes
Cocktail frankfurters
Shrimp
Ham or luncheon meat cubes
Olives
Mushrooms, plain or marinated
Herring
Pickles
Cocktail onions
Smoked oysters
Shrimp 'n Olives (place an olive in the curve of each shrimp)

CHEESY MEATBALLS

1 pound ground beef
¼ cup dry bread crumbs
1 egg
1 cup (4 oz.) shredded Cheddar cheese
½ teaspoon salt
1 teaspoon chili powder
¼ teaspoon pepper

Preheat oven to 350°F. In large bowl, combine all ingredients; blend well. Shape into 1-inch balls. Place in 15x10-inch shallow baking pan. Bake 10 to 12 minutes. Serve hot, on toothpicks.

50 meatballs

HOT OLIVE-CHEESE BALLS

1 cup (4 oz.) shredded
   Cheddar cheese
3 tablespoons butter
   or margarine, softened
½ cup Pillsbury's Best All
   Purpose or
   Unbleached Flour
1 teaspoon paprika
½ teaspoon
   Worcestershire sauce
   Dash cayenne pepper
   Dash salt
24 medium-size olives
   (pitted ripe or stuffed
   green)

Preheat oven to 400°F. Combine cheese and butter. (Lightly spoon flour into measuring cup; level off.) Blend in flour, paprika, Worcestershire sauce, cayenne pepper and salt. Mold a slightly rounded teaspoonful of dough around each olive, covering completely. Place on ungreased cookie sheet. Bake 12 minutes until golden brown.

24 appetizers

TIP: Dough may be refrigerated up to 3 days and used as needed.

HIGH ALTITUDE: No change.

HOT CRABMEAT CANAPÉS

1 cup (7½-oz. can)
   drained crabmeat
½ cup mayonnaise or
   salad dressing
½ teaspoon prepared
   mustard
½ teaspoon
   Worcestershire sauce
1 teaspoon prepared
   horseradish
6 slices bread, toasted
   and crusts removed or
   24 crackers
¼ cup grated Parmesan
   cheese

In small bowl, flake crabmeat. Add mayonnaise, mustard, Worcestershire sauce and horseradish; mix well. Cut each slice of toast into 4 squares. Arrange on cookie sheet. Top each with about 1 tablespoon crab mixture; spread evenly. Sprinkle with Parmesan cheese. Broil 5 to 6 inches from heat until filling is bubbly.

24 canapés

Combine ingredients a day ahead of serving so flavors are thoroughly blended.

TASTY BRAUNSCHWEIGER SPREAD

8-oz. pkg. cream cheese,
   softened
⅓ cup (2 oz.)
   braunschweiger or liver
   sausage
1 to 2 tablespoons
   drained pickle relish
½ to 1 teaspoon
   Worcestershire sauce
¼ teaspoon garlic salt
½ cup (3 oz.) chopped
   peanuts or pecans

In bowl, combine all ingredients except peanuts; blend thoroughly. For easier handling, refrigerate mixture about 15 minutes. Shape mixture into a ball; roll in nuts to coat well. Refrigerate until served. Serve with assorted crackers.

3-inch ball

TIPS: For ONION-FLAVORED BRAUNSCHWEIGER SPREAD, combine 1 envelope (.56 oz.) dry onion dip mix with ¼ cup dairy sour cream; add to cheese mixture.

For BRAUNSCHWEIGER DIP, thin mixture with cream or milk. Use nuts as a garnish.

BACON-WRAPPED WATER CHESTNUTS

8-oz. can water
  chestnuts, drained
¼ cup soy sauce
1 tablespoon sugar
½ pound bacon

Preheat oven to 375°F. Combine water chestnuts (whole or halved), soy sauce and sugar. Marinate about 30 minutes. Drain. Cut bacon slices into thirds; wrap around water chestnuts, fastening with toothpicks. Arrange on broiler pan or on rack in shallow baking pan. Bake 20 to 25 minutes until bacon is crisp. Serve hot.

20 appetizers

BROILED STUFFED MUSHROOMS

16 oz. (2 pt.) large fresh
  mushrooms
2 tablespoons chopped
  onion or 2 teaspoons
  instant minced onion
¼ cup butter or
  margarine
¾ to 1 cup finely chopped
  cooked chicken livers
¼ teaspoon salt
  Dash pepper
1 tablespoon sherry or
  brandy, if desired
2 tablespoons lemon juice
  Melted butter or
  margarine

Remove stems from mushrooms and set aside caps. Finely chop stems. In fry pan, cook onion and chopped mushroom stems in butter until tender. Add chicken livers, salt, pepper and sherry; mix well. Dip mushroom caps in lemon juice and arrange hollow side up in shallow baking pan. Fill with chopped mixture; brush with melted butter. Broil 4 to 5 inches from heat 4 to 5 minutes until heated through and caps are lightly browned. Serve hot.

10 to 12 servings

TIPS: To make ahead, prepare, cover and refrigerate up to 24 hours. Broil just before serving.

May substitute cooked ham for chicken livers; omit salt.

SHRIMP-CHEESE CANAPÉS

¼ cup butter or
  margarine, softened
2 cups (8 oz.) shredded
  Cheddar cheese
1 egg, separated
7 slices bread
28 cooked shrimp

Cream butter and cheese; blend in egg yolk. Beat egg white until stiff; stir into cheese mixture. Trim crusts from bread and cut into canapé shapes. Arrange bread on ungreased cookie sheet. Top each with a shrimp and cover with rounded teaspoonful of cheese mixture. Preheat oven to 350°F. Bake 10 to 12 minutes or until cheese melts.

28 canapés

TIP: To make ahead, assemble, cover and refrigerate up to 12 hours. Bake just before serving.

PARTY SNACK MIX

½ cup butter or
  margarine
1 tablespoon
  Worcestershire sauce
⅛ teaspoon Tabasco sauce
4 cups bite-size shredded
  corn cereal
2 cups bite-size shredded
  wheat cereal
2 cups pretzel sticks
2 cups Spanish peanuts
  or mixed nuts
1 teaspoon salt
¼ teaspoon garlic powder

Melt butter in large shallow baking pan or two 13x9-inch pans. Add Worcestershire and Tabasco. Stir in cereals, pretzels and peanuts. Sprinkle with salt and garlic powder. Toss well. Bake at 325°F. for 25 to 30 minutes, stirring occasionally, until lightly toasted.

3 quarts

TIP: If desired, omit salt and garlic powder; use 1 teaspoon garlic salt.

CHICKEN LIVER PÂTÉ

  1 pound chicken livers
  1½ cups water
  ⅓ cup butter or
    margarine, melted
  1 medium apple, chopped
  1 medium onion, chopped
  1 clove garlic, crushed
    Dash thyme
    Dash marjoram
  ⅓ cup cooking sherry
  ¼ teaspoon salt
    Dash pepper

In saucepan, simmer chicken livers in water 2 to 3 minutes. Drain and reserve ¾ to 1 cup liquid. In fry pan, cook livers in butter until brown. Add apple, onion, garlic, thyme, marjoram, sherry and cooking liquid. Simmer, uncovered, 15 minutes or until liquid is absorbed, stirring occasionally. Grind finely in food chopper or puree in blender. Add salt and pepper. Chill. Serve with Melba toast or crackers.

2 cups

SALMON BALL

  2 cups (16-oz. can)
    drained canned salmon
  8-oz. pkg. cream cheese,
    softened
  1 tablespoon finely
    chopped onion or 1
    teaspoon instant
    minced onion
  ¼ teaspoon salt
  1 tablespoon lemon juice
  1 teaspoon prepared
    horseradish
    Snipped parsley

In bowl, combine all ingredients except parsley; mix well. Refrigerate about 4 hours or until firm enough to shape. Shape mixture into a ball; roll in parsley. Refrigerate at least 1 hour before serving. Serve with crackers or small slices of rye bread.

5-inch ball

TIP: If desired, add ¼ teaspoon liquid smoke.

HOT CHIPPED BEEF DIP

  2 pkg. (8 oz. each)
    cream cheese, softened
  1 cup dairy sour cream
  2 tablespoons milk
  1 tablespoon
    Worcestershire sauce
  ¼ cup instant minced
    onion or ¾ cup finely
    chopped onion
  ¼ cup finely chopped
    green pepper
  2 pkg. (3 oz. each)
    chipped dried beef,
    finely chopped

In large bowl, combine cream cheese, sour cream, milk and Worcestershire sauce. Beat until fluffy. Stir in onion, green pepper and dried beef. Bake at 350°F. for 30 minutes. Serve hot in fondue pot or chafing dish.

4 cups

TANGY CHIPPED BEEF BALL

  8-oz. pkg. cream cheese,
    softened
  ¼ cup dairy sour cream
  1 teaspoon prepared
    horseradish
  ¼ cup grated Parmesan
    cheese
  3-oz. pkg. chipped dried
    beef, finely chopped

In medium bowl, blend cream cheese, sour cream and horseradish until smooth and creamy. Stir in Parmesan cheese and ½ cup dried beef. Refrigerate cheese mixture about 15 minutes for easier handling. Shape cheese mixture into a ball; roll in remaining dried beef. Refrigerate at least 20 minutes or until serving time. Serve with assorted crackers.

4-inch ball

Versatile indeed–use as a dip, a topping for fresh tomatoes or lettuce, or for tacos and tostados.

GUACAMOLE DIP

   1 cup (1 medium) mashed ripe avocado

   2 tablespoons finely chopped onion or 1 teaspoon instant minced onion

   2 tablespoons mayonnaise or salad dressing

   ¼ teaspoon chili powder

   ¼ teaspoon garlic salt

   5 to 6 drops Tabasco sauce

   2 slices crisp bacon, crumbled, or 2 teaspoons imitation bacon-flavored bits

Combine all ingredients except bacon. Refrigerate 30 minutes or until served. Just before serving, add bacon or use as a garnish. Serve with tortilla or corn chips.

TIP: Instead of peeling avocado, cut in half lengthwise, remove pit and scoop fruit out of shell with spoon. Use shells for serving dip.

SOUR CREAM DIPS

Transform sour cream into an easy dip with a few simple flavor additions. Use 1 cup of dairy sour cream or plain yogurt mixed with 2 tablespoons milk.

DEVILED HAM: Add 4½-oz. can deviled ham, 2 tablespoons pickle relish and ¼ teaspoon Worcestershire sauce.

1¾ cups

CHEESE: Add 5-oz. jar processed cheese spread and ¼ teaspoon garlic salt.

1½ cups

ITALIAN: Add 3 tablespoons (1-oz. pkg.) spaghetti sauce seasoning mix.

1 cup

ONION: Add 1 envelope onion salad dressing mix or ½ envelope dry onion soup mix.

1 cup

IDEAS FOR DIPPERS

Chips - potato, taco, corn
Crackers
Melba or rye toast
Pretzels
Bread sticks
Shoestring potatoes
French fried onions
Cauliflowerettes
Radishes
Celery or carrot sticks
Zucchini or cucumber slices
Artichoke hearts
Green pepper strips
Cherry tomatoes
Green onions
Fresh broccoli strips

HOT CLAM DIP

   8-oz. pkg. cream cheese, softened

   6½-oz. can minced clams, drained

   3 tablespoons milk

   2 tablespoons chopped almonds

   1 tablespoon instant minced onion

   1 tablespoon prepared horseradish

   ¼ teaspoon garlic salt

   ¼ teaspoon salt

   Dash pepper

Preheat oven to 375°F. In ovenproof dish, combine all ingredients. Just before serving, bake about 10 minutes or until heated through. Garnish with parsley or paprika.

1½ cups

TIP: This dip is also good served cold. Almonds may be toasted before adding to dip.

Dinners for Two

Flickering candles, an imaginative centerpiece, a beautifully set table and...dinner for two. Sound dramatic? Why not? It's exciting to put forth all your culinary skills for just one special guest. Such cozy, intimate suppers can be every bit as memorable as a full-scale party and often with much less cost and effort. Cooking successfully for two begins at the market when you decide what and how much to buy since you probably don't want leftovers on hand for days afterward. You will notice that in our menu suggestions we have left the larger cuts of meat for other occasions in favor of options that are adaptable to a small-scale party. And since you are entertaining just one person, you will want to select recipes that can be well in hand before the appointed hour of arrival. No guest wants to be "stranded" while the hostess toils in the kitchen. Whether you are celebrating a special occasion or enjoying a quiet "at home" evening, the following palate-pleasers are specially devised to help you enjoy your dinner and your guest to the fullest.

Definitely a celebration-night menu, it gives flair and uniqueness to the favorite steak and baked potato combo. From the colorful fruits glistening in a tasty Honey Dressing (a recipe you will want to use with other fruits as well), to the rich, creamy finalé, every recipe is as deluxe as it is easy to prepare. If you are really splurging, try a dollop of red or black caviar atop the sour cream on the baked potatoes. Serve the dessert in your most decorative champagne glasses or dessert dishes and follow it with demitasse cups of high-quality coffee.

Festive Fillets
Melon Refresher with
Honey Dressing
Bacon-Wrapped Mignons
Salad with
Marinated Artichoke Hearts
Baked Potatoes
Mocha Frappé

MELON REFRESHER WITH HONEY DRESSING

- 1½ cups cantaloupe or honeydew melon balls
- ¼ cup sliced strawberries

Dressing
- ½ cup honey
- ½ cup cooking oil
- 2 tablespoons vinegar
- ½ teaspoon dry mustard
- ½ teaspoon paprika
- ⅛ teaspoon salt
- ½ teaspoon celery seed

Place melon and strawberries in serving dishes or half melon shells. In blender, combine all Dressing ingredients except celery seed; mix well. Stir in celery seed. Spoon dressing over melon just before serving. Store remaining dressing in a covered container in the refrigerator; use for other fruit salads.

2 to 3 servings

The savory butter sauce blends perfectly with the steak's natural juices. Since you are using an expensive cut of meat, watch broiler timings carefully so fillets are cooked to perfection.

BACON-WRAPPED MIGNONS

2 beef tenderloin steaks, 1 to 1½ inches thick
2 slices bacon
1 tablespoon butter or margarine
½ teaspoon parsley flakes or 1 teaspoon snipped parsley
½ teaspoon instant minced onion

Wrap bacon strips around outside of steaks; secure with toothpicks. In small saucepan, melt butter; add parsley and onion. Cook until tender, about 5 minutes. Place steaks on broiler. Broil 3 to 4 inches from heat 5 to 7 minutes on each side for rare, 8 to 10 minutes on each side for medium. Spoon on butter mixture just before serving.

2 servings

TIP: Boneless rib eye steaks may be used in place of tenderloin steaks.

Artichokes are cooked and marinated the night before for little last-minute attention.

SALAD WITH MARINATED ARTICHOKE HEARTS

9-oz. pkg. frozen artichoke hearts
1 small onion, sliced
1 cup prepared Italian dressing
2 tablespoons water
¼ to ½ head lettuce

In saucepan, combine all ingredients except lettuce. Cook as directed on artichoke package. Chill overnight. Tear lettuce into bite-size pieces and place in salad bowl. Add ½ to 1 cup artichoke hearts and some of the marinade. Toss lightly. Store remaining artichoke hearts in a covered container in the refrigerator for use in other salads.

2 to 4 servings

BAKED POTATOES

2 medium baking potatoes

Wash potatoes; prick 2 to 3 times with a fork. If desired, wrap in foil. Bake at 400° F. for 40 to 50 minutes until tender. Using paper towels to protect hands from heat, roll potatoes between hands to make inside potato mixture light and mealy. Make a cross slit on top of potato. Gently press lower part of potato to force potato up through the slit. Top with butter, salt and pepper and/or one of these toppings:
sour cream and chives
crumbled cooked bacon
chopped green onions
crumbled bleu cheese
shredded Cheddar cheese
snipped parsley

2 potatoes

Let your blender do the work for this smoothie!

MOCHA FRAPPÉ

1 pint (2 cups) chocolate ice cream
¼ cup milk
¼ cup creme de cacao
¼ teaspoon instant coffee

Combine all ingredients in blender. Blend until smooth. Pour into serving glasses.

2 (1 cup) servings

TIP: For CREME DE MENTHE FRAPPÉ, use vanilla ice cream and creme de menthe; omit coffee.

No need for cocktails or a soup course—you have the two in one with this mild Sipper laced with sherry. Perfect for Fall and Winter entertaining when there is a chill in the air and a fire blazing indoors. The Cornish Hens bake to tenderness with no last minute fussing, and the need for a salad is eliminated with the Spinach Elegant providing the greenery. The dessert is easily assembled ahead of time to be slipped into the oven minutes before serving. All in all, a delicious meal that leaves a liberated hostess free to enjoy her guest.

After sherry is added, do not allow Sipper to boil again.

BOUILLON SIPPER
  10½-oz. can condensed beef
      bouillon
  ⅔ cup hot water
  2 tablespoons dry sherry

In saucepan, heat bouillon and water to boiling. Stir in sherry. Serve in mugs. If desired, garnish with lemon slices and parsley.

2 (1 cup) servings

Game Hen Gala
Bouillon Sipper
Cornish Game Hen
with Rice Bake
Spinach Elegant
Rum-Baked Bananas

Honey-basted hens become golden brown on a bed of savory rice.

CORNISH GAME HEN AND RICE BAKE
  2 cornish game hens
  ¼ cup wild rice
  ¼ cup long grain white
      rice
  1 teaspoon salt
  ¼ cup chopped celery
  2 tablespoons chopped
      onion
  4-oz. can mushroom
      stems and pieces,
      drained
  1½ cups chicken broth
  2 tablespoons butter or
      margarine
  2 tazlespoons honey

Wash and dry game hens. Using kitchen shears or sharp knife, cut game hens in half lengthwise through breastbone. In 12x8-inch or shallow 2-quart casserole, combine rices, salt, celery, onion, mushrooms, and chicken broth. Dot with butter. Place game hens, cut-side-down, over rice. Brush

with 1 tablespoon honey. Cover with foil and bake at 375° F. for 30 minutes. Uncover; brush game hens with remaining honey. Bake uncovered 30 minutes longer until tender and brown.

2 servings

SPINACH ELEGANT
  10-oz. pkg. frozen spinach
  ½ teaspoon instant minced
      onion or 2 teaspoons
      chopped onion
  ½ teaspoon salt
  Dash pepper
  ¼ cup dairy sour cream

Prepare spinach as directed on package, adding onion, salt and pepper. Drain thoroughly. Stir in sour cream; mix lightly.

2 servings

For best results, select bananas that are firm and just ripe.

RUM-BAKED BANANAS
  2 medium bananas
  3 tablespoons butter or
      margarine
  3 tablespoons brown
      sugar
  ⅛ teaspoon cinnamon
  1 teaspoon rum
  ½ cup whipped topping

Preheat oven to 375°F. Slice bananas lengthwise, then in half, and place in 8-inch pie plate. In small pan, melt butter. Stir in brown sugar and cinnamon. Pour over bananas. Bake 15 to 20 minutes. Fold rum into topping. Spoon sugar sauce over bananas; top with rum-whipped topping.

2 servings

Cornish Game Hen and Rice Bake
Bouillon Sipper

Lamb chops provide welcome variety when cooking for two, and they become a gourmet treat when topped with a mild Sour Cream Sauce. You will find this an especially lovely menu for Spring—just hearty enough for the months when weather is beginning to warm but fresh fruits for the salad are not yet available. The bright yellow and green of the zesty dessert will certainly make you think of daffodils and tulips soon to come.

LAMB CHOPS DELUXE
 2 to 4 lamb chops
 1 tablespoon cooking oil
 1 teaspoon salt
 Dash pepper
 1 small onion, sliced
 ¼ cup water
 1 pkg. sour cream sauce mix
 3 tablespoons water

In large fry pan, brown chops well in oil on both sides. Drain excess fat. Add salt, pepper, onion and ¼ cup water. Cover and simmer 20 to 25 minutes until chops are cooked through. Combine sour cream sauce mix and 3 tablespoons water. Remove chops from pan to heated platter. Stir sour cream sauce into pan drippings. Pour sauce over chops. If desired, garnish with parsley.

2 servings

Spring Fling
Tangy Fruit Salad
Lamb Chops Deluxe
Rice Jardeniere
Minted Orange Peas
Victorian Parfait

When time is short, use quick-cooking rice.

RICE JARDENIÉRE
 Rice for 2 servings
 1 cube or teaspoon chicken bouillon
 1 tablespoon dehydrated vegetables
 ¼ cup cherry tomatoes, quartered

Prepare 2 servings rice, adding chicken bouillon to cooking water. Stir dehydrated vegetables and tomatoes into rice last 10 minutes of cooking. Serve hot.

2 servings

TIP: Two to three tablespoons of finely shredded or chopped carrots, green pepper and onion may be substituted for dehydrated vegetables.

TANGY FRUIT SALAD
 1 cup mixed fruit (chopped apple, pineapple chunks, orange segments, raisins)

 2 tablespoons orange juice or pineapple-orange juice concentrate, thawed
 Lettuce

Toss fruit with orange juice concentrate. Serve on lettuce leaves.

2 servings

Mint—always a favorite accent for both peas and lamb.

MINTED ORANGE PEAS
 10-oz. pkg. frozen peas
 ⅛ teaspoon salt
 ⅛ teaspoon dried mint leaves
 Dash pepper
 2 teaspoons butter or margarine
 2 teaspoons orange marmalade

Cook peas as directed on package; drain. Lightly stir in remaining ingredients. Heat through. If desired, garnish with orange slices.

2 servings

Serve with sugar cookies or another delicately-flavored tea cookie.

VICTORIAN PARFAIT
 1 pint lemon sherbet
 ¼ cup creme de menthe

Alternately spoon sherbet and creme de menthe into parfait or small fancy dessert glasses. Freeze until firm, at least 1 hour.

2 servings

Lamb Chops Deluxe
Rice Jardiniere
Minted Orange Peas

Butter-broiled salmon steaks are enhanced with Spring's first new potatoes, as delicately flavored as the rest of the menu. Begin preparing the cucumbers several hours ahead of serving so they have time to absorb the marinade-dressing. Fruits for the dessert may also be readied ahead so you can give full attention to the timings for the entreé. For the finishing touch and a picture-perfect platter, garnish the salmon with lemon wedges and parsley sprigs.

SALMON STEAKS WITH ZIPPY ITALIAN SAUCE

    2 salmon steaks, about
        ¾-inch thick
    3 tablespoons butter,
        melted
        Salt
        Pepper
    1 pkg. hollandaise sauce
        mix
    ½ cup water
    ⅛ teaspoon Italian
        seasoning

Rinse and dry fish. Brush broiler pan with melted butter. Place fish on broiler pan and brush with melted butter. Season with salt and pepper. Broil 5 to 6 inches from heat for 5 minutes. Turn; brush with melted butter. Continue broiling 5 more minutes. While fish broils, combine hollandaise sauce mix, water and Italian seasoning in small saucepan. Cook, stirring constantly, until thickened.

Salmon Supper Supreme
*Salmon Steaks with
Zippy Italian Sauce
Dilled New Potatoes
Quick Broccoli Dress-Up
Cucumbers in Vinegar and Oil
Fruit Finale*

Remove fish carefully to hot platter and serve with Italian sauce.

2 servings

TIP: Leftover Italian Sauce makes a tasty spread to perk up roast beef sandwiches.

To substitute for Italian seasoning, use ⅛ teaspoon leaf oregano and ⅛ teaspoon leaf basil.

Boil potatoes just until tender so they will hold their shape.

DILLED NEW POTATOES

    4 to 6 (¾ pound) new
        red potatoes
    3 tablespoons butter,
        melted
    2 tablespoons snipped
        parsley
    ⅛ teaspoon dill weed

Lightly scrub potatoes. Pare a band around center of each potato. Cover with water; boil about 30 minutes until tender. Drain. Combine butter, parsley and dill weed. Just before serving, spoon dilled butter mixture over potatoes.

2 servings

Almonds toasted in butter make the easy seasoning for this broccoli.

QUICK BROCCOLI DRESS-UP

    10-oz. pkg. frozen broccoli
        spears
    2 tablespoons butter or
        margarine
    2 tablespoons slivered or
        chopped almonds
    ½ tablespoon lemon juice

Cook broccoli as directed on package; drain. In small saucepan or fry pan, melt butter. Add almonds and cook over medium heat until lightly toasted. Stir in lemon juice. Pour over broccoli in serving dish.

2 to 4 servings

Unpeeled cucumbers scored with fork tines give nice color and added nutrition.

CUCUMBERS IN VINEGAR AND OIL

    ¼ cup cooking oil
    ½ cup vinegar
    2 tablespoons sugar
    ½ teaspoon salt
        Dash pepper
    1 cucumber, thinly sliced
    1 small onion, thinly
        sliced
        Lettuce

In bowl, combine all ingredients except lettuce. Cover and chill 1 to 2 hours. Drain, reserving dressing. Serve on lettuce leaves or toss with lettuce pieces, using oil and vinegar mixture as dressing.

3 to 4 servings

TIP: Cucumbers may be refrigerated in vinegar dressing for several days.

This is an extremely versatile dessert–easy to assemble for entertaining any time of year. If grapes and fresh pineapple are unavailable, canned pineapple or some other fresh fruit substitutes may be used.

FRUIT FINALE

½ cup seedless or seeded grapes, halved

¾ cup drained pineapple chunks

1 cup (1 medium) sliced banana

¼ cup maraschino cherries

1 to 3 tablespoons frozen orange juice concentrate, thawed or orange-flavored liqueur

Half orange shells

In medium bowl, combine all ingredients except orange shells. Chill. Serve fruit mixture in orange shells or sherbet dishes. If desired, garnish with sherbet, fresh mint or lime twist.

2 to 4 servings

Fruit Finale

Fast Feasts

Most of us do one thing when we hear that unexpected company is arriving for dinner--we PANIC! The second thing we are very apt to do is dash to the store and blow the week's budget on a very expensive steak and some costly prepared items to complete the menu — all because we don't feel we have time to cook a meal befitting guests. You will notice that this section is entitled, "Fast Feasts." Why? Because we believe that you can prepare company fare with very short notice and with little more than an hour in the kitchen. Of course, it is helpful if you have an "emergency shelf" with staples that will save you a trip to the store when guests come a-calling, or some tasty tidbits tucked in the freezer just waiting for such an occasion. Even if you are not this organized, the menus here are skillfully designed to be your silent partners in producing sensational meals in record time.

Plain old hot dogs are truly transformed into company fare with a sweet-sour sauce and colorful kabob accompaniments. Have the Butter Bean casserole almost finished baking and the Biscuits oven ready before you begin broiling the kabobs. The recipes are particularly appropriate for summer entertaining when green peppers, tomatoes and cucumbers are at their peak. Keep this menu in mind when children are among the guests because it is loaded with kid-pleasing recipes.

ISLAND FRANK KABOBS

13½-oz. can (1 cup) pineapple chunks (drain and reserve ⅔ cup liquid)
1 pkg. barbecue sauce mix
8-oz. can (1 cup) tomato sauce
1 pound (10) weiners or franks, cut into thirds

Quickie Kabobs
Island Frank Kabobs
Butter Bean Bake
Tomato-Cucumber Salad
Fried Onion Biscuits
Mandarin Orange Whip

1 green pepper, cut into 1-inch squares
10 sweet pickles, cut into 1-inch chunks

In small saucepan, combine ⅔ cup pineapple liquid, barbecue sauce and tomato sauce. Heat, stirring occasionally, until mixture boils. Thread wieners, pineapple, green pepper and pickle alternately on 10 skewers. Broil or grill 2 to 3 inches from heat, brushing frequently with sauce. Broil 3 to 4 minutes on each side until heated through and lightly browned.

4 to 6 servings

The flavor of fried onions makes these biscuits especially tempting with barbecued meats.

FRIED ONION BISCUITS

½ cup chopped onion
2 tablespoons butter or margarine
8-oz. can Pillsbury Refrigerated Buttermilk or Country Style Biscuits

Preheat oven to 425°F. In small fry pan, sauté onions in butter until tender. Separate biscuit dough into 10 biscuits; dip each into pan to coat both sides with onions and butter. Arrange in ungreased 8 or 9-inch round pan. Spoon remaining onions and butter over biscuits. Bake 9 to 12 minutes until golden brown. Serve warm.

10 biscuits

HIGH ALTITUDE: No change.

Two types of beans plus diced bacon add variety to this easy casserole.

BUTTER BEAN BAKE

3 slices bacon, diced
¼ cup chopped celery
16-oz. can (2 cups) pork and beans
16-oz. (2 cups) butter beans, drained
2 tablespoons brown sugar
2 teaspoons prepared mustard

In medium fry pan, fry bacon until crisp. Remove from pan. Add celery and cook until tender. Reserve 1 tablespoon bacon. Add bacon and remaining ingredients. Stir gently. Turn into 1½ to 2-quart casserole. Top with reserved bacon. Bake at 375°F. for 20 to 25 minutes.

4 to 6 servings

An extremely attractive meal with an exceptional array of textures, flavors and bright colors. With the pie quickly prepared beforehand to allow for chilling, the rest of the menu can be table ready in less than an hour. Your guests will never believe this was a spur-of-the-moment supper!

If you are substituting fruit juice for the port, try orange or pineapple juice or apricot nectar.

PORT-GLAZED HAM

½ cup Port wine or fruit juice
¼ cup firmly packed brown sugar or honey
1 smoked ham slice, cut 1½-inches thick

Island Frank Kabobs, p. 103
Fried Onion Biscuits, p. 103
Tomato-Cucumber Salad
Butter Bean Bake

TOMATO-CUCUMBER SALAD

½ cup salad dressing or mayonnaise
2 tablespoons vinegar or lemon juice
¼ teaspoon salt or garlic salt
¼ teaspoon leaf oregano or Italian seasoning
2 to 3 tomatoes, diced
1 cucumber, diced

In medium bowl, combine first 4 ingredients. Add tomatoes and cucumbers; toss lightly. Refrigerate until serving time.

4 to 6 servings

Hurry-Up Ham

Port-Glazed Ham
Tropical Tater Bake
Peas with Mushrooms and Onions
Sour Cream Coleslaw
Limelight Pie

Combine wine and brown sugar in measuring cup. Place ham slice on rack in broiler pan. Broil or grill 4 to 5 inches from heat, basting frequently with wine mixture. Broil 12 to 15 minutes on each side.

4 to 6 servings

Experiment with other favorite fruits and yogurt flavors, too.

MANDARIN ORANGE WHIP

2 cups prepared whipped topping
1 cup (8-oz. carton) orange flavored yogurt
11-oz. can (1 cup) mandarin orange sections, drained
Macaroon crumbs or chopped nuts to garnish

In medium bowl, combine whipped topping and yogurt; stir until thoroughly mixed. Fold in orange sections. Spoon into serving dishes. Garnish with macaroon crumbs or nuts. Chill in freezer 30 minutes; do not freeze until solid. Move to refrigerator if serving time is later.

4 to 6 servings

PEAS WITH MUSHROOMS AND ONIONS

4-oz. can mushroom stems and pieces, drained
¼ cup (½ small) chopped onion or 1 tablespoon instant minced onion
2 tablespoons butter or margarine
2 cups (10-oz. pkg. or 16-oz. can) peas, cooked and drained
¼ teaspoon salt
Dash pepper
Dash ground allspice

In small saucepan, sauté mushrooms and onion in butter until tender. Add remaining ingredients. Serve immediately.

4 servings

Combining ingredients just before serving will give you a delightfully crisp texture.

SOUR CREAM COLESLAW

    1 small head cabbage, shredded or thinly sliced
 1½ teaspoons instant minced onion or 2 tablespoons finely chopped onion
    2 tablespoons sugar
    ½ teaspoon salt
    ½ cup dairy or imitation sour cream
    1 teaspoon lemon juice

In large bowl, combine all ingredients; toss lightly. Serve immediately.

4 servings

This menu is as delicious as it is quick to prepare. Begin by making the dessert, since it should chill while you complete the rest of the meal. You may also wish to ready the salad greens and store them in the refrigerator until serving time. Remember that proper carving of the London Broil is essential for tenderness — across the grain and then into very thin slices.

Pop this under the broiler along with the ham when the ham is just a few minutes away from being done.

TROPICAL TATER BROIL

 18-oz. can sweet potatoes or yams, drained
    2 bananas, peeled and cut into quarters
    ¼ cup firmly packed brown sugar
    ¼ cup corn syrup
    2 tablespoons butter or margarine

Arrange potatoes and bananas in single layer in pan with sides for broiling. In small saucepan, combine remaining ingredients. Heat, stirring occasionally, until butter has melted. Pour syrup mixture over potatoes and bananas, coating well. Broil 4 to 5 inches from heat for 5 to 8 minutes until heated through and lightly

Swift Steak

*London Broil with
Mushroom-Tomato Sauce
Poppy Cheese Noodles
Crispy Onion and Greens Toss
Speedy Bread Sticks
Banana Cream Parfaits*

browned on top. Spoon syrup mixture over potatoes and bananas to serve.

4 to 5 servings

LIMELIGHT PIE

    8-inch baked pastry shell
 14-oz. can sweetened condensed milk
    ⅓ cup lime juice
    ¼ teaspoon salt
    8-oz. can (⅔ cup) crushed pineapple, drained
    2 to 4 drops green food coloring
       Whipped cream

In small bowl, combine condensed milk, lime juice and salt; stir until thickened. Blend in pineapple and food coloring. Spread in baked pastry shell. Chill 2 to 3 hours. Serve with whipped cream.

8-inch pie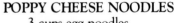

POPPY CHEESE NOODLES

    3 cups egg noodles
    ¾ cup (3 oz.) shredded American cheese
    1 teaspoon poppy seeds

Prepare noodles as directed on package. Drain. Stir in cheese and poppy seed. Cover; let stand 2 to 3 minutes. (Heat from noodles will melt cheese.) Serve hot.

6 servings

Peas with Mushrooms and Onions, p. 105
Sour Cream Coleslaw
Port Glazed Ham, p. 105
Tropical Tater Broil

A robust sauce adds unique flavor and heartiness to this grilled favorite.

LONDON BROIL WITH MUSHROOM-TOMATO SAUCE

1½ pounds flank steak
Sauce
  ½ cup (1 medium) sliced onion
  1 tablespoon butter or margarine
10¾-oz. can condensed golden mushroom soup
  ⅓ cup chopped canned tomatoes
  ⅓ cup tomato liquid or water
  2 tablespoons snipped parsley or 1 tablespoon parsley flakes
  1 tablespoon Dijon mustard or ½ tablespoon prepared mustard

Prepare Sauce before grilling steak. In saucepan, cook onion in butter until tender. Add remaining ingredients. Heat, stirring occasionally. Keep warm to serve over sliced meat. Place steak on grill 3 to 4 inches from hot coals. Grill 5 minutes on each side for medium rare. Thinly slice meat diagonally across the grain. Serve with Sauce.

6 servings

SPEEDY BREAD STICKS

8-oz. can Pillsbury Country Style or Buttermilk Refrigerated Biscuits
1 egg white, slightly beaten
Coarse salt

Preheat oven to 400°F. Cut each biscuit in half. Roll into pencil shape, 4 to 6 inches long. Place on greased cookie sheet; brush with beaten egg white. Sprinkle with salt. Bake 12 to 15 minutes until golden brown.

20 bread sticks

TIP: Use caraway, sesame, or poppy seed or Parmesan cheese for coarse salt, if desired.

HIGH ALTITUDE: No change.

No slicing or chopping of onions for this speedy salad.

CRISPY ONION AND GREENS TOSS

  3 cups iceberg lettuce, torn into bite-size pieces
  3 cups fresh spinach, torn into bite-size pieces
  ½ cup French fried onion rings
  ¼ cup prepared French or other colorful dressing

In salad bowl, toss lettuce and spinach with part of onion rings. (Reserve remainder for garnish.) Chill until ready to serve. Top with dressing and reserved onion rings.

6 servings

This no-bake dessert will remind you of Banana Cream Pie without the high-calorie crust. Remember to keep pudding mixes on hand for quick, nutritious treats.

BANANA CREAM PARFAITS

  1 pkg. (4-serving size) instant vanilla pudding mix
  2 cups milk
  2 cups vanilla wafers
  2 bananas, sliced

Prepare vanilla pudding with milk as directed on package. Layer vanilla wafers, banana slices and pudding in parfait glasses or individual serving dishes. Repeat layering, ending with pudding. If desired, garnish with whipped topping or shredded coconut. Refrigerate for 30 to 45 minutes until ready to serve.

6 servings

TIP: For SNAPPY APRICOT PARFAITS, use gingersnaps for vanilla wafers and a 17-oz. can apricot halves, drained, for bananas.

If you happen to be a fisherman, this menu is sure to become one of your all-time favorites. Even with a purchased "catch," the secret of the delicious breading makes it almost as tasty as freshly caught. Because fish cools so quickly, try to have a heated serving platter ready to keep it piping hot until it reaches the table. The meal ends with a real scene-stealer — an elegant Grasshopper dessert that chills quickly in the freezer and adds a festive note to the simplest of meals.

Fisherman's Luck
Golden Fried Fish
Cauliflower Scramble
Citrus-Avocado Salad
Corny Bread Muffins
Grasshopper Dessert Pudding

A few herb additions to the golden breading make a delicious difference.

GOLDEN FRIED FISH
      2 pounds fish fillets or steaks
      1 cup cracker meal, toasted bread crumbs or corn meal
      2 teaspoons parsley flakes
      ¼ teaspoon ground thyme
      ¼ cup milk
         Cooking oil or shortening
         Salt
         Pepper

Wash and dry fish. In shallow pan or plastic bag, combine cracker meal, parsley and thyme. Mix well. Dip fish in milk, then in cracker meal mixture; coat both sides. In large fry pan, cook fish in hot oil 2 to 3 minutes per side until crisp and golden. Season with salt and pepper. Fish should flake easily with a fork when done. Drain on paper toweling. Serve on heated platter. If desired, garnish with lemon wedges and serve with tartar sauce.

4 servings

CAULIFLOWER SCRAMBLE
      10-oz. pkg. cauliflower in cheese sauce
      1 medium zucchini squash
      2 tablespoons chopped onion
      1 tablespoon butter or margarine
      ½ teaspoon salt
      1 tomato, cut into 8 wedges

Cook cauliflower as directed on package. In saucepan, cook zucchini and onion in butter until tender. Stir in cauliflower and remaining ingredients. Heat through.

4 servings

Serve plain or drizzle each salad with colorful French dressing.

CITRUS-AVOCADO SALAD
      1 ripe avocado
         Lemon juice
      1 orange or grapefruit
         Lettuce leaves

Peel, seed and slice avocado; sprinkle with lemon juice to prevent browning. Peel and section orange. On salad plates lined with lettuce, alternate avocado slices and orange sections.

4 servings

CORNY BREAD MUFFINS
      ½ cup Pillsbury's Best All Purpose or Unbleached Flour
      ½ cup yellow corn meal
      2 teaspoons sugar
      2 teaspoons baking powder
      ¼ teaspoon salt
      ½ cup milk
      2 tablespoons cooking oil
      1 egg
      ½ cup whole kernel corn, drained

Preheat oven to 400°F. (Lightly spoon flour into measuring cup; level off.) In bowl, combine first five ingredients. Add milk, oil and egg. Beat with rotary beater about 1 minute until smooth. Stir in corn. Fill 10 greased (not oiled) or paper-lined muffin cups ½ to ⅔ full. Bake 15 to 20 minutes until lightly browned.

10 muffins

HIGH ALTITUDE — above 3500 Feet: Reduce baking powder to 1½ teaspoons. Bake at 425°F. for 15 to 20 minutes.

Keep this in mind for holiday suppers. The color makes it perfect!

GRASSHOPPER DESSERT PUDDING

⅔ cup crushed chocolate
  wafers
1 pkg. (4-serving size)
  instant vanilla pudding
2 cups milk

2 tablespoons créme de
  menthe
1 tablespoon créme de
  cacao

Spread ⅓ cup crushed wafers over bottom of 1-quart dish; reserve remainder for topping. Prepare pudding with milk as directed on package; stir in créme de menthe and créme de cacao. Spoon pudding over crumbs. Sprinkle on remaining crumbs. Chill in freezer 30 minutes. Do not freeze until solid; move to refrigerator if serving time is later. To serve, spoon into parfait or wine glasses.

4 servings

Grasshopper Dessert Pudding

Seasonal Entertaining

Seasonal parties have inherent success features which need only a bit of dramatizing and organization on the part of the hostess to make an eagerly-awaited event a memorable occasion. For the religious holidays, we usually bow to long-established family traditions, adding a few personal touches of our own to reflect favorite aspects of the occasion. As for the other gatherings— Valentine's Day, Oktoberfest, St. Patrick's Day and your own special rite of Spring, we embellish the existing theme with dashes of originality and accents of imagination. People the world over love to assemble to commemorate seasonal events. No doubt, that common bond of joyful anticipation which offers a reason for a party in the first place usually helps make our entertaining a grand success.

Ring in the "New" with a sparkling open house and a buffet table laden with a sumptuous holiday buffet. Since it's only once a year, we've splurged a bit with Champagne Punch, deluxe appetizers and a choice of elegant Stroganoffs to please the most discerning gourmet guests. Don't be discouraged by a lengthy-looking menu. Many of the items are do-ahead numbers, and only one appetizer requires heating. Rely on a chafing dish to keep the Stroganoff at just the right temperature and let the eager guests help themselves when the clock strikes "time to eat."

Holiday "spirits" are sparked with gay red berries.

CHAMPAGNE ROSÉ PUNCH

2½ cups (two 10-oz. pkg.) frozen, sweetened strawberries, thawed

6½ cups (two ⁴/₅-quart bottles) rosé wine, chilled

6-oz. can frozen lemonade concentrate, thawed

3¼ cups (⁴/₅-quart bottle) champagne, chilled

Ice cubes

New Year's Eve Buffet

Champagne Rosé Punch
Broiled Shrimp Appetizers
Cheese Neapolitan
Marinated Crab Meat
Chutney Egg Spread
Julienne Beets
Dilled Cucumbers
Chicken Livers Stroganoff
OR
Beef Stroganoff
Holiday Cinnamon-Apple Mold
Eggnog Cake with Fruit Sauce
Café Brûlot

In large bowl, combine strawberries and 3¼ cups (one ⁴/₅ quart) rosé wine. Cover; let stand at room temperature 1 hour. Press strawberry mixture through strainer into punch bowl or 3-quart container; add thawed lemonade concentrate, remaining rosé wine, champagne and ice cubes, mixing well. Serve immediately.

26 (½ cup) servings

TIP: Wines vary in sweetness so taste punch and add sugar if necessary.

BROILED SHRIMP APPETIZERS

10-oz. pkg. frozen cooked shrimp, thawed and chopped

¼ cup mayonnaise or salad dressing

2 tablespoons finely chopped green pepper

½ teaspoon curry powder

About 16 crackers

⅓ cup shredded natural Swiss cheese

In bowl, combine shrimp, mayonnaise, green pepper and curry powder. Spoon onto crackers, spreading to edges. Top with cheese. Broil about 6 inches from heat 1 to 2 minutes until cheese is melted.

16 appetizers

A do-ahead, layered beauty for special occasions.

CHEESE NEAPOLITAN

1st layer
> 2 pkg. (3 oz. each) cream cheese, softened
> ½ cup grated Bel Paese cheese
> ½ cup snipped parsley

2nd layer
> 2 pkg. (3 oz. each) cream cheese, softened
> 2 tablespoons tomato paste or catsup
> 2 tablespoons grated Parmesan cheese
> ¼ teaspoon basil leaves
> ½ teaspoon sugar

3rd layer
> 2 pkg. (3 oz. each) cream cheese, softened
> ⅛ teaspoon garlic powder
> Dash onion salt
> ½ cup Ricotta cheese
> Snipped parsley
> Crackers

In bowl, blend first three ingredients; spread in bottom of 3-cup mold or crock lightly oiled and lined with plastic wrap extending up over edges. Chill while preparing 2nd layer. Blend 2nd layer ingredients. Spread evenly over first layer. Chill. Blend first three ingredients for 3rd layer; stir in Ricotta cheese. Spread evenly over 2nd layer. Cover with foil. Chill overnight to blend flavors. To unmold, lift out, holding edges of plastic wrap; invert on plate. Peel off wrap. Sprinkle with chopped parsley. Serve with crackers.

2½ cups

Serve a variety of these goodies with crackers for a colorful array of "appeteasers."

MARINATED CRAB MEAT

> 2 tablespoons mayonnaise
> 1 tablespoon chili sauce
> 1 teaspoon lemon juice
> 7½-oz. can crab meat, drained and flaked

In bowl, blend first three ingredients; stir in crab meat. Cover and chill. Serve with crackers.

1⅓ cups

CHUTNEY EGG SPREAD

> 2 cups dairy sour cream
> 1 hard-cooked egg, finely chopped
> 1½ tablespoons finely chopped chutney
> 1 tablespoon finely chopped celery
> 1 teaspoon lemon juice
> ½ teaspoon salt
> ⅛ teaspoon black pepper

In bowl, combine all ingredients; mix well. Cover and chill. Serve with crackers.

2 cups

DILLED CUCUMBERS

> 2 tablespoons olive or cooking oil
> 1 tablespoon cider vinegar
> ½ teaspoon dried dill weed
> 1 cucumber, scored and sliced

In small bowl, blend first three ingredients; pour over cucumber slices. Cover and chill.

1½ cups

JULIENNE BEETS

> 16-oz. jar pickled beets, drained and cut into slivers
> ¼ cup dairy sour cream
> 2 tablespoons finely chopped onion

In bowl, combine all ingredients. Cover and chill.

1¾ cups

BEEF STROGANOFF

> 2 pounds sirloin or round steak, cut into thin strips
> 8 oz. (2 cups) fresh mushrooms, sliced
> 2 medium onions, sliced
> 2 tablespoons cooking oil
> 2 cubes or teaspoons beef bouillon
> 1 cup hot water
> ½ teaspoon salt
> 2 tablespoons tomato paste or catsup
> 1 teaspoon dry or 2 teaspoons prepared mustard
> 2 tablespoons flour
> ½ cup water
> ½ to 1 cup dairy sour cream
> 4 to 6 cups cooked rice or egg noodles

In large fry pan, sauté steak, mushrooms and onions in hot oil until golden brown. Add bouillon, water, salt, tomato paste and mustard. Cover; simmer about 20 minutes (45 minutes for round steak) until tender. Combine flour and water. Stir into meat mixture. Heat to boiling, stirring constantly; boil 1 minute. Reduce heat; stir in sour cream. Heat, but do not boil. Serve over hot rice or noodles.

6 servings

TIP: Dry red wine or sherry may be used for half of water.

CHICKEN LIVERS STROGANOFF

1 pound chicken livers
2 tablespoons butter or margarine
½ teaspoon ground oregano
½ teaspoon Worcestershire sauce
1 small onion, chopped
2 tablespoons flour
½ teaspoon salt
⅛ teaspoon pepper
4-oz. can undrained mushroom stems and pieces
¼ cup dry white wine
¼ cup dairy sour cream
4 to 6 cups cooked rice

Cut chicken livers in half. In large fry pan, heat butter with oregano and Worcestershire sauce. Add livers and onion; brown slowly over medium heat, 5 to 7 minutes.

Remove livers from pan; set aside. Blend in flour, salt, pepper and mushrooms. Heat to boiling, stirring constantly; boil 1 minute. Return livers to pan. Add wine. Cover and simmer 3 to 5 minutes. Stir in sour cream, mixing well. Heat through; do not boil. Serve over hot rice.

4 to 6 servings

Chicken Livers Stroganoff

HOLIDAY CINNAMON-APPLE MOLD

½ cup red cinnamon candies
1 cup boiling water
3-oz. pkg. lemon-flavored gelatin
1¼ cups thick sweetened applesauce
8-oz. pkg. cream cheese, softened
½ cup salad dressing or mayonnaise
½ cup chopped nuts
½ cup chopped celery

In saucepan, heat cinnamon candies in boiling water until dissolved, stirring constantly. Add gelatin; stir to dissolve. Stir in applesauce. Pour half of gelatin mixture into 9x5-inch loaf pan; chill until firm. Cool remaining gelatin until slightly thickened. In bowl, combine cream cheese with salad dressing; add nuts and celery. Spread over firmly set gelatin. Pour remaining gelatin over cheese layer; chill until firm. Cut in slices to serve.

6 servings

EGGNOG CAKE WITH FRUIT SAUCE

1 pkg. Pillsbury Plus Yellow Cake Mix
3 eggs
¼ cup cooking oil
¼ cup rum
1 cup whipping cream
½ teaspoon nutmeg

Fruit Sauce

⅓ cup firmly packed brown sugar
1 tablespoon cornstarch
1 pound, 13 oz. can fruit cocktail, sliced peaches or apricot halves, drained (reserve syrup for sauce)
¼ teaspoon almond extract
¼ cup butter or margarine

Preheat oven to 350° F. Grease (not oil) and flour 12-cup fluted tube pan (non-stick finish pan, too). In large bowl, blend first six ingredients until moistened. Beat 2 minutes at highest speed. Pour into prepared pan. Bake 35 to 45 minutes until toothpick inserted in center comes out clean. Cool upright in pan 5 minutes; turn onto serving plate. Cool completely. In medium saucepan, blend brown sugar and cornstarch. Stir in reserved syrup, extract and butter. Bring to full boil over medium heat, stirring constantly; boil 1 minute. Remove from heat; stir in fruit. Serve over cut pieces of cake.

10-inch ring cake

HIGH ALTITUDE:

A flaming finale for the most festive of parties.

CAFÉ BRÛLOT

2 orange peels, cut into thin strips
2 lemon peels, cut into thin strips
2 tablespoons sugar
1 stick cinnamon
12 whole cloves
1 cup cognac
¼ cup curacao
1 quart strong black coffee

In brûlot bowl or deep chafing dish, combine first five ingredients and mash together with ladle or large spoon. Add heated cognac and curacao; ignite. Gradually add coffee. Stir lightly until flame disappears. Serve in goblets or mugs.

5½ cups

A sweetheart of a menu for a sentimental holiday, featuring Valentine red throughout. With such a delightful theme, how simple it is to tie it all together with special Valentine invitations, a hearts-and-flowers centerpiece and romantic dinner music to highlight the occasion. Every recipe is loaded with eye-appeal and portions of each course for this red-letter day can be partially prepared in advance. The party has a splendid beginning with a hot, spicy punch, perfect for a chilly February evening, and it ends with a choice of two show-off desserts. Guests will "eat up" your very tasty way of wishing them "Happy Valentine's Day."

A terrific punch to serve over the Christmas holidays, too.

ROSY CIDER BOWL
Whole cloves
1 large orange
1½ quarts apple cider
1 pint cranberry juice
⅓ cup lemon juice

Insert cloves, about ½-inch apart, into orange. Place in shallow pan; bake at 350°F. for 30 minutes. In saucepan, combine apple cider and cranberry juice. Heat until small bubbles form around edges. Remove from heat; stir in lemon juice. Pour into heat-proof punch bowl. Pierce orange in several places with two-pronged fork; float in cider mixture. Serve in mugs or heat-proof punch cups.

16 (½ cup) servings

Valentine Dinner Party
Rosy Cider Bowl
Wine and Cheese Ball
Easy Veal Paprika
OR
Creole Pork Steaks
Confetti Beans
Vegetable Cocktail Aspic
Heart Cake
OR
Cherry Crescent
Cheesecake Cups

WINE AND CHEESE BALL
4-oz. cream cheese, softened
1½ tablespoons Port wine or dessert sherry
½ tablespoon prepared mustard
1 tablespoon minced onion
2 cups (8 oz.) shredded Cheddar cheese
¼ cup chopped nuts

In bowl, combine all ingredients except nuts. Form into ball. Cover and refrigerate. Just before serving roll in nuts. Serve with knife and crackers.

3-inch ball

EASY VEAL PAPRIKA
2 tablespoons flour
½ teaspoon salt
Dash pepper
1 pound boneless veal, cut into cubes
2 tablespoons oil
1¼ cups water
½ to 1 tablespoon paprika
6¼-oz. pkg. noodles with sour cream and cheese sauce mix
⅓ cup water
½ cup milk
1 tablespoon butter or margarine

In plastic bag, combine flour, salt and pepper. Add veal cubes; shake to coat. In large fry pan, brown meat in hot oil. Add 1¼ cups water and paprika. Cover and simmer 45 minutes or until meat is tender. Add package of noodles and ⅓ cup water. Continue simmering, covered, 10 minutes until noodles are cooked, stirring occasionally. In bowl, combine milk, butter and package of sauce mix; stir to mix well. Pour over veal and noodle mixture. Simmer until sauce thickens and boils, stirring gently. If desired, garnish with parsley.

4 to 6 servings

CREOLE PORK STEAKS

    4 to 6 pork steaks, or
      chops (about 2 pounds)
    1 stalk celery, sliced
    15-oz. can tomato sauce
    1½ cups water
    2 tablespoons brown
      sugar
    1 teaspoon salt
    ¼ to ½ teaspoon leaf
      basil
    1 cup uncooked long
      grain or quick-cooking
      white or brown rice

Grease bottom of large fry pan with small piece of pork fat. Brown steaks over medium heat, turning once. Add celery; brown slightly. Drain excess fat. Combine remaining ingredients; add to fry pan. Cover and simmer 30 minutes (40 minutes for brown rice) until rice and steaks are tender. Add water, if necessary.

4 to 6 servings

A quickie dress-up for a favorite vegetable.

CONFETTI BEANS

    9-oz. pkg. frozen wax
      beans
    ½ to 1 pkg. (3 oz.)
      low-calorie or regular
      cream cheese, cubed
    ¼ cup chopped green
      pepper
    2 tablespoons chopped
      pimento

Cook beans as directed on package; drain well. Add remaining ingredients; mix well. Serve immediately.

4 servings

VEGETABLE COCKTAIL ASPIC

    1¾ cups vegetable juice
      cocktail
    3-oz. pkg. lemon flavored
      gelatin
    ½ cup finely chopped
      celery
    ½ cup shredded carrot
    1½ teaspoons lemon juice
      Dash salt

In small saucepan, bring vegetable juice cocktail to boil; remove from heat. Add gelatin and stir until dissolved. Add remaining ingredients. Pour into 3-cup mold or 8-inch square pan. Chill until firm, about 4 hours. To serve, unmold or cut into squares.

4 servings

HEART CAKE

Prepare your favorite flavor Pillsbury Plus Cake Mix as directed on package. Pour batter into one 8 or 9-inch round layer pan and one 8 or 9-inch square pan (both should be 8 or 9-inch, not one of each). Bake as directed. Cool completely. Cut round in half to form 2 semi-circles, fitting cut edges to adjoining sides of square. Frost with double recipe of favorite frosting, making sure that top and sides are completely covered.

1 heart cake

One of our prettiest BAKE-OFF® entries ever.

CHERRY CRESCENT CHEESECAKE CUPS

    2 pkg. (3 oz. each)
      cream cheese, softened
    1 egg
    1 cup powdered sugar
    ¼ cup chopped nuts
    1 teaspoon almond extract
    8-oz. can Pillsbury
      Refrigerated Quick
      Crescent Dinner Rolls
    1 cup (½ of 21-oz. can)
      prepared cherry pie
      filling
    2 tablespoons lemon
      juice or kirsch
    ½ tablespoon butter or
      margarine

Preheat oven to 350°F. Grease eight muffin cups. In large bowl, combine cream cheese and egg until smooth. Stir in powdered sugar, nuts and extract; mix well. Unroll crescent dough into four 6x4-inch rectangles. Firmly press perforations to seal. Pat out each to 10x5-inch rectangle. Cut into eight 5-inch squares. Place scant ¼ cup cream cheese mixture in center of each square. Bring four corners of square to center. Place filled squares, sealed-side-up, in greased muffin cups. Bake 18 to 22 minutes until golden brown. Immediately remove from pan. In small saucepan, combine pie filling, lemon juice and butter. Cook over low heat until butter melts and mixture boils. Serve over warm cheesecake cups.

8 desserts

HIGH ALTITUDE: No change.

Even if you didn't hail from the old sod, you will want to join in the wearin' o' the green and invite over some friends for a hearty March celebration. You won't need the luck of the Irish to handle this one—everything is so easy and the "stew-pendous" main dish will be assembled and simmering long before company calls. A shamrock special from start to finish, the menu features traditional flavors of potatoes, corned beef and lamb, and the color of the evening is emerald green, to be sure. Why not follow dessert with mugs of Irish Coffee (page 53) topped with puffs of rich whipped cream?

EMERALD ISLE PUNCH
    1 pint lime sherbet
    1 quart ginger ale, chilled

Place small spoonfuls sherbet in punch cups or bowl. Pour in ginger ale. Serve immediately.

10 (½ cup) servings

These snacks are also great with soup for wintertime lunches.

CORNED BEEF BITES
    ¾ cup (3 oz.) sliced corned beef, chopped
    ½ cup (2 oz.) shredded Cheddar cheese
    ¼ cup mayonnaise or salad dressing
    2 tablespoons pickle relish

St. Pat's Party
Emerald Isle Punch
Corned Beef Bites
Dublin Stew
Sunshine Salad Bowl
Whole Wheat Potato Bread
OR
Potato Chive Rolls
Chocolate Pistachio Cake

    ½ teaspoon instant minced onion
    ½ teaspoon Worcestershire sauce
    10-oz. can Hungry Jack® Refrigerated Big Flaky Biscuits
    1 egg, slightly beaten Sesame seeds or poppy seeds

Preheat oven to 375°F. Grease 20 small muffin cups. In large bowl, combine first six ingredients; mix well. Separate biscuit dough into 10 biscuits; separate each biscuit into 2 layers. Press each biscuit to 3-inch circle. Spoon 1 tablespoon filling onto each biscuit. Fold dough over filling, covering completely; seal well. Place in greased muffin cups. Brush with egg; sprinkle with sesame seed. Bake 15 to 20 minutes until golden brown. Remove from pan while warm. Serve warm.

20 snacks

HIGH ALTITUDE: No change.

DUBLIN STEW
    2 pounds boneless lamb, cut into cubes
    ½ teaspoon sugar
    1 tablespoon cooking oil
    2 teaspoons salt
    ½ teaspoon pepper
    ⅓ cup flour
    2 cups water
    ¾ cup dry red wine
    1 clove garlic, minced
    1 teaspoon Worcestershire sauce
    6 to 8 carrots, peeled and cut into pieces
    4 small whole onions, quartered
    4 stalks celery, cut into pieces
    2 to 3 potatoes, peeled and cut into pieces

Sprinkle meat with sugar. In large fry pan or Dutch oven, brown meat on all sides in hot oil. Stir in salt, pepper and flour. Add water, wine, garlic and Worcestershire sauce. Cover; simmer 45 minutes or until meat is tender, stirring occasionally. Add vegetables; cover and cook 30 to 45 minutes until vegetables are tender.

5 to 6 servings

TIP: If desired, omit wine and use 2¾ cups water.

SUNSHINE SALAD BOWL

½ cup cooking oil
⅓ cup frozen orange juice
    concentrate, thawed
⅓ cup honey
2 tablespoons vinegar
1½ teaspoons salt
1½ teaspoons sugar
1 teaspoon dry mustard
1 teaspoon paprika
    Dash pepper
5 cups torn salad greens
11-oz. can (1 cup)
    mandarin oranges,
    drained
1 small onion, thinly
    sliced and separated
    into rings

Combine first nine ingredients in container with tightly fitted cover. Cover; shake well. Chill. Reserve a few orange sections and onion rings for garnish. In large salad bowl, combine greens, oranges and onion rings. Add dressing; toss lightly.

5 to 6 servings

Mashed potato flakes help create this hearty, wholesome favorite.

WHOLE WHEAT POTATO BREAD

1½ cups water
1¼ cups milk
¼ cup butter or
    margarine
¼ cup honey
3½ cups Pillsbury's Best
    All Purpose or
    Unbleached Flour*
1½ cups Hungry Jack®
    Mashed Potato Flakes
2½ teaspoons salt
2 pkg. active dry yeast
2 eggs
2½ to 3 cups Pillsbury's
    Best Whole Wheat
    Flour

In large saucepan, heat first four ingredients until very warm (120°F. to 130°F.). (Lightly spoon flour into measuring cup; level off.) In large bowl, combine warm liquid, 2 cups all-purpose flour, potato flakes, salt, yeast and eggs; beat 4 minutes at medium speed. By hand, stir in remaining flours. On well-floured surface, knead dough until smooth and elastic, about 5 minutes. Place in greased bowl. Cover; let rise in warm place until light and doubled in size, 45 to 60 minutes. Generously grease (not oil) two 9x5 or 8x4-inch loaf pans. Punch down dough; divide and shape into 2 loaves. Place in greased pans. Cover; let rise in warm place until light and doubled in size, 30 to 45 minutes. Preheat oven to 375°F. Bake 35 to 40 minutes until deep golden brown and loaves sound hollow when lightly tapped. If loaves become too brown, loosely cover with foil last 10 minutes of baking. Immediately remove from pans. If desired, brush with butter or margarine.

2 loaves

*If using Pillsbury's Best Self-Rising Flour, omit salt.

HIGH ALTITUDE: No change.

These light and airy pull-apart rolls are mildly flavored with sour cream and chives.

POTATO CHIVE ROLLS

2 cups milk
½ cup dairy sour cream
5 to 5½ cups Pillsbury's
    Best All Purpose or
    Unbleached Flour*
1 tablespoon sugar
3 teaspoons salt
2 to 4 teaspoons
    chopped chives
1 cup Hungry Jack®
    Mashed Potato Flakes
2 pkg. active dry yeast
2 eggs

In small saucepan, heat milk and sour cream until very warm (120°F. to 130°F.). (Lightly spoon flour into measuring cup; level off.) In large bowl, combine warm liquid, 2 cups flour and remaining ingredients; beat 4 minutes at medium speed. By hand, stir in remaining flour. Cover; let rise in warm place until light and doubled in size, 45 to 60 minutes. Generously grease (not oil) 13x9-inch pan. On well-floured surface, toss dough until no longer sticky. Divide dough into 24 pieces; shape into balls. Place in greased pan. Cover; let rise in warm place until light and doubled in size, 30 to 45 minutes. Preheat oven to 375°F. Bake 25 to 30 minutes until golden brown. Immediately remove from pan. If desired, lightly dust tops of rolls with flour.

24 rolls

*Self-rising flour not recommended.

HIGH ALTITUDE: No change.

A rich, pistachio-flavored pound cake with a chocolate ripple inside. Beautiful color and appearance.

CHOCOLATE PISTACHIO CAKE

    1 pkg. Pillsbury Bundt Pound
       Cake Supreme Mix
    1 pkg. (4-serving size) instant
       pistachio pudding and pie
       filling
    1½ cups water
    ¼ cup butter or margarine,
       softened
    3 eggs
    ¾ cup chocolate syrup

Preheat oven to 350° (325° for colored fluted tube pan). Using solid shortening or margarine (not oil), grease 12-cup fluted tube pan (non-stick finish pan, too). In large bowl, combine Packet 1 (base mix), Packet 2 (pound mix) and remaining ingredients except chocolate syrup; blend on low speed until moistened. Beat 2 minutes at medium speed (portable mixer at highest speed). Pour 4 cups of batter into prepared pan. To remaining batter, add chocolate syrup; blend well. Pour chocolate batter over batter in pan. Bake 55 to 75 minutes or until toothpick inserted in center comes out clean. Cool upright in pan 45 minutes; turn onto serving plate. Cool completely. Sprinkle Packet 3 (topping) over cool cake. 10-inch ring cake.

HIGH ALTITUDE—5200 Feet: Bake at 350° for 65 to 75 minutes.

Easter Dinner

Cream of Leek Soup
Baked Ham
Sherried Pear Salad
Parslied Potatoes
Springtime Asparagus
Hot Cross Buns
Grasshopper Soufflé

The traditional Easter favorites are here in all their glory—golden glazed ham, hot cross buns plus tender, fresh asparagus. And just to add the spice of variety, we've included some novel food finery for this Springtime feast. The menu discards the hearty and the heavy of the winter past in favor of a lighter touch, pastel shades and the harvest of early gardens to grace your table. The popular entrée is easily prepared to allow extra time for you to make the soup, rolls, salad and spectacular dessert soufflé. We wouldn't be surprised if this Easter menu became a family tradition at your house.

From the onion family come milder, delicious leeks.

CREAM OF LEEK SOUP

    4 to 6 medium leeks or large
       green onions
    6 tablespoons butter or
       margarine
    3 tablespoons flour
    2 teaspoons chopped chives
    ½ teaspoon salt
    6 cups milk or light cream
    6 cubes or teaspoons chicken
       bouillon

Thinly slice leeks, discarding top green portion. In saucepan over medium heat, cook leeks in butter 8 to 10 minutes or until tender, stirring occasionally. Stir in flour, chives, and salt; add milk and bouillon. Cook over medium heat, stirring occasionally, until soup boils 1 to 2 minutes. Garnish servings with nutmeg, if desired.

6 (1 cup) servings

BAKED HAM

Place ham, fat-side-up, on rack in shallow roasting pan. Insert meat thermometer so bulb reaches center of thickest part but does not rest in fat or on bone. (Do not add water; do not cover.) Bake as directed in Timetable. About 15 minutes before ham is done; remove from oven. Pour drippings from pan. If necessary, trim fat, leaving only thin layer on ham. Score ham by cutting diamond shapes about ¼-inch deep through fat. If desired, insert whole clove in each diamond. Spoon one of suggested glazes over ham; return to oven and bake 15 to 20 minutes more.

Allow about 3 to 4 servings per pound

TIMETABLE FOR BAKED HAM

Ham	Weight	Meat Thermometer Reading	Approximate Cooking Time Per Pound
(Cook-before-eating)			
Whole ham	10-14 lbs.	160° F.	18-20 minutes
Half ham	5-7 lbs.	160° F.	22-25 minutes
Shank or butt portion	3-4 lbs.	160° F.	35-40 minutes
Picnic shoulder	5-8 lbs.	170° F.	35 minutes
(Fully cooked or canned)			
Whole ham	10-14 lbs.	130° F.	10-15 minutes
Half ham	5-7 lbs.	130° F.	18-24 minutes
Shank or butt portion	3-4 lbs.	130° F.	18-24 minutes
Picnic shoulder	5-8 lbs.	130° F.	25-30 minutes

A perfect accompaniment for your holiday ham.

SHERRIED PEAR SALAD

1 pound, 13-oz. can pear halves or slices, drained (reserve ½ cup syrup)
½ cup firmly packed brown sugar
1 tablespoon chopped crystallized ginger or ¼ teaspoon ground ginger
¼ teaspoon cinnamon
½ cup dry sherry
2 tablespoons vinegar
Lettuce
Chopped walnuts

In small saucepan, combine ½ cup reserved pear syrup with brown sugar, ginger, cinnamon, sherry and vinegar. Stir over medium heat until sugar is dissolved; pour over pears. Cover; chill overnight or for several days. To serve, remove pears from liquid, arrange on lettuce, garnish with walnuts.

6 servings

TIPS: Liquid may be used again. Pears can also be served as dessert. Top with whipped cream or cream cheese.

PARSLIED POTATOES

1½ to 2 pounds new potatoes, cooked, drained and peeled
¼ cup butter or margarine
1 to 2 tablespoons snipped parsley or parsley flakes
⅛ teaspoon celery salt or seasoned salt, if desired

In same saucepan used to cook potatoes, melt butter; stir in parsley and celery salt. Add potatoes; toss lightly.

4 to 6 servings

TIP: Two cans (16 oz. each) small whole or sliced potatoes can be used for new potatoes.

GLAZES FOR BAKED HAM

Brown Sugar Glaze: Combine 1 cup firmly packed brown sugar, 2 tablespoons flour, ½ teaspoon prepared mustard, ⅛ teaspoon cinnamon and 3 tablespoons dry sherry, vinegar or water; mix well. Spread on ham.

Jelly Glaze: Heat 1 cup currant or apple jelly until melted. Spread on ham.

Orange Marmalade Glaze: Spread 1 cup orange marmalade on ham.

Pineapple Glaze: Combine 1 cup firmly packed brown sugar with ¾ cup drained, crushed pineapple; spread on ham.

The first Spring sprouts of asparagus take on an oriental flair.

SPRINGTIME ASPARAGUS

2 pounds fresh asparagus, cut into ½-inch pieces
2 tablespoons cooking oil
⅛ teaspoon pepper
⅛ teaspoon ground ginger
2 tablespoons soy sauce
8-oz. can water chestnuts, drained and sliced

In fry pan, cook asparagus in oil until tender, about 5 minutes. Add remaining ingredients; heat through, stirring constantly.

6 servings

HOT CROSS BUNS

- 1 pkg. Pillsbury Hot Roll Mix
- ¾ cup warm water
- 1 egg
- ½ cup currants or raisins
- 3 tablespoons chopped citron, if desired
- 1 teaspoon cinnamon
  Soft butter or margarine

Frosting

- ½ cup powdered sugar
- 1½ teaspoons butter or margarine, softened
- 1 teaspoon milk or light cream
- ¼ teaspoon vanilla

Prepare hot roll mix with water and egg as directed on package, adding currants, citron and cinnamon with the flour mixture.

Cover; let rise in warm place until doubled in size, 45 to 60 minutes. Grease (not oil) 8 or 9-inch square pan. On well-floured surface, toss dough lightly until no longer sticky. Divide dough into 16 equal portions and shape into round balls. Place in greased pan. Cover; let rise until doubled in size, 30 to 45 minutes. Preheat oven to 375° F. Bake 20 to 25 minutes until golden brown. Brush with soft butter; cool slightly. To prepare Frosting, stir all ingredients together in small bowl until of spreading consistency. Form frosting cross on top of each bun with decorating tube.

16 buns

HIGH ALTITUDE: No change.

Hot Cross Buns

Make this dessert in a large soufflé dish for a buffet or in individual dishes for a formal dinner party.

GRASSHOPPER SOUFFLÉ

- ¼ cup sugar
- 1 envelope (1 tablespoon) unflavored gelatin
  Dash salt
- 1 cup milk
- 3 eggs, separated
- 3 tablespoons creme de cacao
- 3 tablespoons green creme de menthe
- ¼ cup sugar
- 1 cup whipping cream, whipped or 2 cups (4½-oz. pkg.) frozen whipped topping, thawed

Prepare 3 to 4-cup soufflé dish or 5 to 6 individual soufflé dishes by forming collar of wax paper around top of dish that extends about 3 inches above dish. (Greasing inside upper edge of dish holds paper in place.) In medium saucepan, combine ¼ cup sugar with gelatin and salt. Stir in milk; blend well. Beat egg yolks (reserve whites in small bowl); add to milk mixture. Cook over medium heat, stirring constantly, until mixture just begins to bubble. Remove from heat. If mixture is not smooth, beat with rotary beater. Stir in creme de cacao and creme de menthe. Refrigerate until mixture is thickened but not set. Beat egg whites until frothy. Gradually add ¼ cup sugar, beating until mixture forms stiff peaks. Fold into gelatin mixture along with whipped cream. Pour into prepared dish. Refrigerate 4 hours or until served. If desired, serve topped with whipped cream.

6 servings

Spring is spelled with a menu like this one! When the weather begins to warm and we're on the threshold of a new season, our mouths water for fresh new potatoes, a savory roast of Spring lamb and a lighter-than-air dessert. We scan the marketplace for the first fresh fruits and vegetables of the season. This menu would be perfect for Easter Day or any other special Springtime occasion.

SPRING FRUIT COCKTAIL

1 cup drained pineapple chunks
1 cup orange sections
¾ cup fresh or frozen melon balls
2 bananas, sliced
1 cup fresh strawberries, whole or sliced
¼ cup lemon juice
2 to 4 tablespoons sugar or honey

Combine fruit. Blend lemon juice and sugar. Spoon over fruit and chill. If desired, garnish with mint leaves.

4 to 6 servings

LAMB ROAST

Place roast, fat side up, on rack in shallow roasting pan. Season with salt and pepper. Insert meat thermometer so bulb reaches the center of thickest part of meat, being sure bulb does not rest in fat or on bone. (Do not add water; do not cover.) Roast to desired degree of doneness using Timetable for Roasting Lamb.

Allow about 2 to 3 servings per pound

Springtime Special
Spring Fruit Cocktail
Seasoned Roast of Lamb
Creamed Garden Potatoes and Peas
Frozen Strawberry Salad
Ambrosia Bread
Chilled Lemon Soufflé

GLAZES FOR LAMB ROAST

Garlic Glaze: Combine ⅓ cup dry sherry, ⅓ cup water, 1 tablespoon paprika, ½ teaspoon leaf basil, 2 tablespoons soy sauce, 2 tablespoons oil and 3 cloves garlic, minced. Brush lamb with Glaze every 30 minutes during roasting.
Jelly Glaze: Melted ¾ cup mint, currant or apricot muscatel jelly over low heat. Brush on lamb during last hour of roasting.

Spicy Glaze: Combine ¼ cup firmly packed brown sugar, 1 clove garlic, minced, 1½ teaspoons salt, ½ teaspoon dry mustard, ½ teaspoon chili powder, ¼ teaspoon ground ginger, ¼ teaspoon ground cloves and 1 tablespoon lemon juice. Brush on lamb during last hour of roasting.

HOW TO CARVE LEG OF LAMB

Place leg of lamb on platter with shank to carver's right. Remove several slices from thin side to form solid base on which to set roast. Turn roast on its base. Starting at shank end, remove a small wedge cut; then carve perpendicular to leg bone. Release slices by cutting under them and along leg bone, starting at shank end. For additional servings, turn over to original position and make slices to the bone. Release and serve.

Timetable for Roasting Lamb to Medium Doneness*

Cut	Weight	Meat Thermometer Reading	Approximate Cooking Time Per Pound
Leg (bone in)	3-5 lbs.	180°F.	35-40 minutes
Leg (bone in)	5-8 lbs.	180°F.	30-35 minutes
Leg (boneless)	3-5 lbs	180°F.	35-40 minutes
Crown Roast	4-6 lbs.	180°F.	40-45 minutes
Rib (rack)	2-3 lbs.	180°F.	40-45 minutes
Shoulder (bone in)	4-6 lbs.	180°F.	30-35 minutes
Shoulder (cushion-style)	3-5 lbs.	180°F.	30-35 minutes
Shoulder (rolled)	3-5 lbs.	180°F.	40-45 minutes

*For lamb medium rare, cook to 155° to 160° on meat thermometer, decreasing cooking time 5 minutes per pound.

Garnish this frosty favorite with mint leaves or whole, fresh strawberries.

FROZEN STRAWBERRY SALAD

8-oz. pkg. cream cheese, softened
2 tablespoons mayonnaise or salad dressing
1 tablespoon lemon juice
10-oz. pkg. (1¼ cups) frozen strawberries, partially thawed
1 cup whipped topping or whipped cream

In medium bowl, blend cream cheese until smooth and creamy. Add mayonnaise; mix well. Beat in lemon juice and strawberries, ¼ cup at a time (so mixture will not curdle). Fold in whipped topping. Pour into 8-inch square pan, ice tray or individual molds; freeze until firm, about 4 hours. Serve on lettuce. If desired, garnish with mint leaves.

6 servings

Frozen Strawberry Salad

The addition of dill makes a delicious difference.

CREAMED GARDEN POTATOES AND PEAS

1 pound small, early red
  potatoes
2 tablespoons butter or
  margarine
1 tablespoon chopped
  onion
2 tablespoons flour
1¼ teaspoons salt
½ teaspoon dill weed
⅛ teaspoon pepper
1½ cups milk
1½ cups fresh or 10-oz.
  pkg. frozen peas, cooked

Cook unpeeled potatoes in boiling water until tender, 20 to 25 minutes. Drain and cool enough to handle; peel if desired. Set aside. In same saucepan, combine butter and onion. Cook until onion is tender. Blend in flour, salt, dill and pepper. Stir in milk, mixing well. Cook until mixture boils, stirring constantly. Boil 1 minute. Add potatoes and peas. Heat through.

4 to 5 servings

TIP: When early potatoes are not available, use about 4 medium potatoes. Cook and cut into pieces before adding to sauce.

AMBROSIA BREAD

1 egg
1 cup water
1 pkg. Pillsbury Apricot
  Nut Bread Mix
8-oz. can (¾ cup) crushed
  pineapple, drained
½ cup flaked coconut

Preheat oven to 350°F. Grease (not oil) and flour bottom only of 8x4 or 9x5-inch loaf pan. In large bowl, combine egg and water. Add nut bread mix, pineapple and coconut. Stir 50 to 75 strokes or until thoroughly combined. Turn into prepared pan. Bake 55 to 65 minutes until toothpick inserted in center comes out clean. Cool 20 minutes; remove from pan.

1 loaf

HIGH ALTITUDE: Follow adjustments on package.

They just can't say "no" to this delectable company dessert.

CHILLED LEMON SOUFFLÉ

½ cup sugar
1 envelope (1 tablespoon)
  unflavored gelatin
¼ teaspoon salt
1 cup water
3 eggs, separated
1 tablespoon grated fresh
  lemon peel or ½
  tablespoon prepared
  lemon peel
3 to 4 tablespoons lemon
  juice
⅓ cup sugar
1 cup whipping cream,
  whipped

Prepare 3 to 4-cup soufflé dish or 5 to 6 individual soufflé dishes by forming a collar of waxed paper around top of dish that extends about 3 inches above dish. (Greasing inside upper edge of dish holds paper in place.) In medium saucepan, combine ½ cup sugar with gelatin and salt. Stir in water. Beat egg yolks (reserve whites in small bowl); add to gelatin mixture. Cook over medium heat, stirring constantly, just until mixture begins to bubble. Remove from heat. If mixture is not smooth, beat with rotary beater. Stir in lemon peel and juice. Cool until mixture is thickened but not set. Beat egg whites until frothy. Gradually add ⅓ cup sugar, beating until mixture holds stiff peaks. Fold into gelatin mixture along with whipped cream. Pour into prepared dish. Refrigerate 4 hours or until served. Carefully remove waxed paper before serving.

5 to 6 servings

A stout-hearted menu for robust appetites and a harvest time celebration. Certainly a theme that lends itself beautifully to the casual approach—a gay buffet table, a keg of icy cold beer and perhaps, strains of German folk music oom-pah-pahing in the background. Create a rathskeller atmosphere in your recreation room and decorate with bold, warm colors and German steins filled with dried Fall arrangements. And don't forget to greet your guests with a hearty "Wilkommen!"

If good-quality bratwurst is not readily available where you shop, see if your grocer can order it for you in time for the party.

BEER AND BRATWURST

1 pound (6 to 8) bratwurst or other smoked sausage
1 to 2 cans (12 oz. each) beer
2 medium onions, sliced
1 teaspoon celery seed, if desired
1 bay leaf, if desired
1 tablespoon butter or margarine

In covered saucepan, gently simmer bratwurst, beer, onion, celery seed and bay leaf 5 minutes. Remove from heat; let stand until ready to grill. Drain off liquid. Grill or broil bratwurst 3 to 4 inches from heat, about 3 minutes on each side. Fry onions in butter until tender; serve with bratwurst.

4 to 5 servings

Sauerkraut and Bean Slaw
German Potato Salad
Beer and Bratwurst

Oktoberfest

*Beer and Bratwurst
German Potato Salad
Sauerkraut and Bean Slaw
Broiled Tomatoes
with Mustard Topping
Toffee Treasure Cake*

This unusual, tangy slaw doubles as a relish, too.

SAUERKRAUT AND BEAN SLAW

16-oz. can sauerkraut, drained
8-oz. can sliced green beans, drained
½ cup chopped onion
¼ cup shredded carrot
2 tablespoons diced green pepper
⅔ cup sugar
½ cup vinegar

In large bowl, combine first five ingredients. In small saucepan, combine sugar and vinegar; bring to boil. Pour over sauerkraut mixture; stir to combine. Cover; refrigerate overnight.

3 cups

BROILED TOMATOES WITH MUSTARD TOPPING

4 to 5 tomatoes
Salt
Pepper
¼ cup mayonnaise or salad dressing
2 tablespoons prepared or ½ teaspoon dry mustard

3 tablespoons chopped onion or 1 tablespoon instant minced onion

Cut tomatoes in half; sprinkle with salt and pepper. Combine mayonnaise, mustard and onion; spread on tomato halves. Place in shallow baking pan. Bake at 350°F. for 15 minutes; then broil 2 to 3 minutes or until golden brown.

4 to 5 servings

The potatoes should still be warm in order to fully absorb the sweet-sour sauce flavors.

GERMAN POTATO SALAD

4 medium potatoes
4 slices bacon
1 small onion, chopped or 6 green onions, sliced
2 tablespoons sugar
1 tablespoon flour
1 teaspoon or cube beef bouillon
1 teaspoon salt
¼ teaspoon ground allspice, if desired
Dash pepper
¼ cup vinegar
½ cup water

Cook unpeeled potatoes. In fry pan, fry bacon until crisp; drain on paper towels, reserving 3 tablespoons drippings. Crumble bacon. To reserved drippings add onion; cook until tender. Add sugar, flour, bouillon and spices; stir until smooth. Stir in vinegar and water; bring to boil. Peel warm potatoes; slice and add to sauce mixture with bacon. Toss lightly to coat. Serve warm.

4 to 5 servings

TIP: If serving is delayed, place salad in covered casserole in oven set at 300°F.

TOFFEE TREASURE CAKE

- ¼ cup sugar
- 1 teaspoon cinnamon
- 2 cups Pillsbury's Best All Purpose or Unbleached Flour*
- 1 cup sugar
- 1½ teaspoons baking powder
- 1 teaspoon soda
- ¼ teaspoon salt
- 1 teaspoon vanilla
- 1 cup dairy sour cream
- ½ cup butter or margarine, softened
- 3 eggs
- ¼ cup chopped nuts
- 6 (⅝ oz. each) or 3 (1⅛ oz. each) chocolate-toffee candy bars, coarsely crushed

Preheat oven to 325°F. (300°F. for colored fluted tube pan). Grease (not oil) and flour 12-cup fluted tube pan (non-stick finish pan, too). Combine ¼ cup sugar with cinnamon; set aside. (Lightly spoon flour into measuring cup; level off.) In large bowl, combine remaining ingredients except nuts and candy bars. Blend at low speed until moistened; beat 3 minutes at medium speed, scraping bowl occasionally. Spoon 2 cups batter into prepared pan. Sprinkle with 2 tablespoons cinnamon-sugar mixture. Spoon remaining batter into pan. Sprinkle with remaining cinnamon-sugar mixture, then with nuts and crushed candy bars. Bake 50 to 60 minutes until toothpick inserted in center comes out clean. Cool upright in pan 5 minutes; turn onto serving plate. Cool completely. If desired, sprinkle with powdered sugar.

10-inch ring cake

*For use with Pillsbury's Best Self-Rising Flour, omit baking powder, soda and salt.

TIP: To easily crush candy bars, place in plastic bag in freezer about 5 minutes to harden.

HIGH ALTITUDE — above 3500 Feet: Bake at 350°F. for 35 to 40 minutes.

Toffee Treasure Cake

A few changes here and there, but really not much different from the first harvest feast for which our Pilgrim forefathers and Indian friends gave thanks. We present a classic menu—as colorful as Jack Frost's paintbox, as bountiful as the old-fashioned groaning board and featuring, of course, Tom Turkey and all the trimmings. It is a tribute to the first settlers that we have kept their culinary traditions alive—no one really desires or expects a menu which departs much from the standard favorites. However, you may wish to experiment with a variety of stuffings for your golden bird and why not try our tempting suggestions for the vegetables and dessert? Although the meal honors years past, it offers the hostess of today the convenience of refrigerated and frozen foods—a welcome change from that first Thanksgiving.

A refreshing "starter" for a heavy meal.

FALL FRUIT COCKTAIL

2 cups grapefruit sections, cut into thirds
1 medium apple, quartered, cored and sliced
2 cups orange sections, halved (4 medium oranges)
1 cup cooked pitted prunes
2 bananas, sliced
¼ cup lemon juice
¼ cup sugar or honey

In bowl, combine all ingredients. Chill.

6 to 8 servings

New England Thanksgiving Feast

Fall Fruit Cocktail
Roast Turkey
Bread Stuffing
Almond-Rice Stuffing
Mashed Potatoes and Gravy
Baked Squash with Orange
Green Beans Supreme
Cranberry-Orange Relish
Hot Butterflake Rolls
Pumpkin-Nog Pie

ROAST TURKEY

1 turkey
Stuffing for turkey (See table for amount needed)
Melted butter or margarine, to baste

Thaw turkey, if frozen; remove giblets from body cavity. Rinse, drain and dry bird. Rub cavity lightly with salt, if desired. Loosely stuff neck area; fasten neck skin to back with skewer. Stuff body cavity lightly (dressing expands); close cavity with skewers and lace with string. Fold wings to back of bird by lifting a wing up and out and forcing the tip back until it rests flat against the back; tie drumsticks to tail. Place, breast side up, on rack in shallow roasting pan. Brush skin with melted butter or margarine. If meat thermometer is used, insert so bulb is in center of inside thigh muscle or thickest part of breast, not touching bone. Cover with loose tent of foil or lay piece of cheesecloth or muslin (moistened with melted butter or margarine) over top and side of bird to prevent excessive browning. If desired, baste or brush entire turkey or dry areas occasionally with pan drippings or melted butter. Bake at 325°F. until meat thermometer registers 180°F. or drumstick gives readily when moved up and down. When ⅔ done, cut string or band of skin between drumsticks and tail to release legs and permit heat to reach thick meat part. If more browning is desired, remove foil or cheesecloth during last hour of roasting.

Allow 1 to 2 servings per pound
TIPS: Stuff turkey just before roasting; do not stuff turkey the night before.

To roast turkey in large brown paper bag, place stuffed turkey in bag, folding end or pinning it. Place on large pan (with edges to catch drippings). Place on lowest rack in oven. **Do not** allow bag to touch electric coils of oven. Bake at 325°F. according to chart.

APPROXIMATE TIMETABLE FOR ROAST TURKEY*

Allow 1 to 2 servings per pound

	Average Weight (pounds)	Amount of Stuffing (quarts)	Meat Thermometer Reading		Approx. Roasting Time at 325°F. (hours)
			Meat	Stuffing	
	4-6	1-1½	180-185°F.	165°F.	2-3
	6-8	1½-2	180-185°F.	165°F.	3-3½
Turkey—	8-12	2-3	180-185°F.	165°F.	3½-4½
Whole	12-16	3-4	180-185°F.	165°F.	4½-5½
	16-20	4-5	180-185°F.	165°F.	5½-6½
	20-24	5-6	180-185°F.	165°F.	6½-7
	3½-5	1-1½	180-185°F.	165°F.	3-3½
Turkey—	5-8	1½-2	180-185°F.	165°F.	2½-3
Halves and	8-10	2-2½	180-185°F.	165°F.	3-3½
Quarters	10-12	2½-3	180-185°F.	165°F.	3½-4

*Times will be slightly less for unstuffed birds and rotisserie roasting.

Try this new stuffing for this year's turkey. Wild rice is especially festive.

ALMOND-RICE STUFFING

½ cup butter or
    margarine
¼ cup chopped onion
4 cups cooked rice (white,
    brown, wild or
    combination)
½ cup chopped or slivered
    almonds
1 teaspoon poultry seasoning
1 teaspoon salt

In fry pan, cook butter and onion until tender, stirring occasionally. Mix in cooked rice, almonds, poultry seasoning and salt.

1 quart stuffing

TIP: Cooked seasoned rice mixes may be substituted for rice; omit poultry seasoning and salt.

Some people prefer a very moist dressing, while others prefer not to add any liquid. Add a little at a time until desired moistness is reached.

BREAD STUFFING

½ cup butter or
    margarine
1 medium onion,
    chopped
2 stalks celery, chopped
8 cups dry bread cubes
2 tablespoons snipped
    parsley, if desired
1 teaspoon salt
2 tablespoons poultry
    seasoning, ground sage
    or savory
¼ teaspoon pepper
    About ½ cup broth or
    water*

In fry pan, cook butter, onion and celery until tender, stirring occasionally. In large bowl, combine bread cubes, parsley, salt, poultry seasoning and pepper. Mix to combine. Add liquid and butter-onion mixture, stirring until desired moistness (dressing will become a little more moist during cooking because it absorbs juices from bird).

2 quarts stuffing

*Broth can be chicken bouillon dissolved in water or cooking liquid from giblets.

TIPS: Day-old soft bread cubes can be used for dry bread cubes. Reduce broth to about ¼ cup.

If desired, add 1 beaten egg before adding broth.

FOR NUT STUFFING, add ½ cup chopped nuts—almonds, filberts, pecans, walnuts or peanuts. For a toasted flavor, cook nuts with onion mixture.

FOR SESAME STUFFING, cook ¼ cup sesame seed with onion mixture.

FOR APPLE-RAISIN STUFFING, add 2 medium apples, peeled and chopped, and ⅔ cup raisins. (Apples will make dressing more moist, so reduce liquid by 2 tablespoons.)

MASHED POTATOES

8 medium peeled potatoes, cooked
1 teaspoon salt
¼ cup butter or margarine
4 to 6 tablespoons milk

Drain cooked potatoes. Mash. Add remaining ingredients except milk; gradually add milk, beating until light and fluffy. If desired, top with additional butter and sprinkle with pepper or paprika.

6 to 8 servings

GRAVY

2 cups hot liquid (broth, water or milk)
¼ cup poultry drippings
¼ cup flour
½ cup cold liquid
Salt
Pepper

Add hot liquid to drippings in roasting pan. Combine flour and cold liquid; mix until smooth. Add flour mixture to hot liquid, stirring constantly. Cook until mixture thickens and boils. Boil 1 minute, stirring constantly. Season with salt and pepper.

2½ cups gravy

TIP: If gravy lumps, beat with beater or wire whip, or strain before serving.

HOT BUTTERFLAKE ROLLS

2 cans (8 oz. each) Pillsbury Refrigerated Quick Butterflake Dinner Rolls
Egg white, slightly beaten
Poppy or sesame seed

Prepare rolls as directed on label; brush with egg white and sprinkle with seed before baking. Serve hot.

12 rolls

GREEN BEANS SUPREME

2 pkg. (10 oz. each) frozen green beans
2 tablespoons butter or margarine
1 medium stalk celery, sliced
¼ cup slivered almonds
1 teaspoon salt
Dash pepper

In saucepan, cook beans as directed on package. Drain. In medium saucepan, fry celery and almonds in butter 10 minutes or until celery is tender and almonds lightly browned. Add beans, salt and pepper; toss lightly. Heat through.

6 to 8 servings

A soufflé-like casserole with the added zest of marmalade.

BAKED SQUASH WITH ORANGE

2 pkg. (12 oz. each) frozen cooked squash
2 eggs, slightly beaten
6 tablespoons orange marmalade
1 teaspoon lemon juice
1 tablespoon butter, melted
⅓ cup (8 crackers) saltine cracker crumbs

Cook squash as directed on package. Stir in egg, marmalade and lemon juice. Place in 1½-quart casserole. Combine butter and crumbs; sprinkle over squash. Bake at 350° F. for 20 minutes.

6 to 8 servings

CRANBERRY-ORANGE RELISH

1 pound (4 cups) cranberries
1 medium orange, cut up
1 medium apple, quartered
¾ cup sugar

Grind cranberries, unpeeled orange and unpeeled apple using blender, food chopper or grinder. Add sugar; mix well. Chill.

4 cups

TIPS: Best if made day before so flavors blend.

Relish can be frozen.

PUMPKIN NOG PIE

1 cup Pillsbury's Best All Purpose or Unbleached Flour
½ teaspoon salt
½ teaspoon pumpkin pie spice
½ cup solid shortening
3 to 4 tablespoons cold water

Filling
16-oz. can (2 cups) pumpkin pie filling
1 cup prepared eggnog* (reserve 2 tablespoons for Topping)
2 eggs

Topping
½ cup cold milk
Reserved eggnog
½ teaspoon vanilla
1 envelope dessert topping mix

Preheat oven to 400°F. In medium bowl, combine flour, salt, and pumpkin pie spice. Cut in shortening, using pastry blender or two knives, until mixture is size of small peas. Sprinkle water over mixture, one tablespoon at a time, while tossing and mixing lightly with a fork. Add water until dough is just moist enough to hold together. Shape into a ball;

flatten slightly on lightly-floured pastry canvas or board. With stockinette-covered or lightly-floured rolling pin, roll out dough to a circle 1½ inches larger than inverted 9 or 10-inch pie pan. Fold pastry in half; place in pie pan. Unfold dough and fit loosely into pan, pressing out air pockets. Trim pastry 1 inch from rim of pie pan; turn edge under to form a standing rim and flute. Preheat oven to 400°F. (375°F. for glass pan). In medium bowl, combine Filling ingredients; beat until smooth. Pour Filling into pastry-lined pan. Bake 45 to 50 minutes until knife inserted near center comes out clean. Cool. In small bowl, combine Topping ingredients; beat until peaks form, about 2 minutes. To serve, spoon Topping around edge of pie. (Refrigerate any leftovers.)

9-inch pie

*To substitute for prepared eggnog, use 1 cup light cream or evaporated milk and ¼ teaspoon each nutmeg and rum flavoring.

HIGH ALTITUDE—above 3,500 Feet: Reduce shortening to ⅓ cup. Bake as directed.

Pumpkin Nog Pie, p. 133
Steamed Christmas Pudding, p. 138
Lemon Sauce, p. 138
Cherry Crescent Cheesecake Cups, p. 118
Grasshopper Souffle, p. 124
Chocolate-Pistachio Cake, p. 122

" 'Tis the season to be jolly," even if you are the one in charge of this year's traditional Christmas feast for the assembled clan. With a magnificent crown roast in the spotlight, this menu is designed for the hostess who wants to enjoy all the festivities of the day along with her family and still be assured that a spectacular meal will be ready at the appointed hour. Beginning with the warm, fragrant Wassail Bowl and continuing throughout this elegant dinner, many items can be assembled the day before and safely stored in the refrigerator or freezer. So, decorate your table in its Christmas best and sit back with your holiday guests and savor each glamorous course of this memorable meal.

WASSAIL BOWL
Whole cloves
1 large orange
8 cups (2 quarts) apple juice or cider
3 tablespoons lemon juice
4 cinnamon sticks

Insert cloves, about ½ inch apart, into orange. Place in shallow pan; bake at 350°F. for 30 minutes. Pierce orange in several places with 2-pronged fork. In large saucepan, combine apple juice, lemon juice, cinnamon sticks and baked orange. Simmer, covered, over low heat for 30 minutes. Remove cinnamon sticks and orange. Pour into heatproof punch bowl. Float clove-studded orange in punch bowl. Serve hot.

16 (½ cup) servings

Christmas
Wassail Bowl
Stuffed Shrimp
Cranberry-Stuffed
Crown Roast of Pork
Broccoli with Lemon Sauce
Double Corn Scallop
Daiquiri Fruit Salad
Steamed Christmas Pudding
with Sauces

Wassail Bowl

The "crowning touch" for any gala occasion.

CRANBERRY-STUFFED PORK CROWN ROAST
7-pound pork crown roast
1½ teaspoons salt
¼ teaspoon pepper

Cranberry Stuffing
4 cups dry bread cubes
1½ cups chopped cranberries
¼ cup sugar
2 tablespoons finely chopped onion or 2 teaspoons instant minced onion
2 tablespoons grated orange peel
1 teaspoon salt
½ teaspoon leaf marjoram
¼ teaspoon leaf thyme
½ cup butter or margarine, melted
½ cup orange juice

For easy carving, have meat man cut off backbone. Season meat with salt and pepper. Place in roasting pan, rib bones up. Wrap tips of bones in foil to prevent excess browning. Insert meat thermometer so bulb reaches center of thickest part but does not rest in fat or on bone. (Do not add water; do not cover.) Roast on lowest oven rack at 325°F. for 2 hours. Meanwhile prepare Cranberry Stuffing. Combine all stuffing ingredients; toss lightly. Fill center of roast with stuffing and roast 1½ to 2 hours longer, until meat thermometer registers 170°F. Cover stuffing with foil if top becomes too brown. To serve, remove foil and cover bone ends with paper frills or spiced crabapples.

6 to 8 servings

TIP: If desired, use seasoned bread cubes for stuffing, omitting salt, marjoram and thyme.

This elegant appetizer may be prepared and refrigerated up to 12 hours ahead of serving.

STUFFED SHRIMP

  2 tablespoons Roquefort
    or bleu cheese, softened
  1 oz. cream cheese,
    softened
  1 tablespoon mayonnaise
    or salad dressing
  ½ teaspoon leaf thyme,
    crushed
  ½ teaspoon paprika
  ½ teaspoon lemon juice
  1 pound cooked, cleaned
    large shrimp
  ¼ cup snipped parsley

Blend softened cheeses with mayonnaise, thyme, paprika and lemon juice. Cut shrimp in half lengthwise and place ½ teaspoon filling between halves. Dip edge in parsley. Refrigerate about 30 minutes to set cheese. Serve with cocktail picks.

About 15 large shrimp

TIP: For a petite and less costly appetizer, sandwich two small shrimp together with ½ teaspoon filling between them.

About 40 small shrimp

May prepare ahead and refrigerate up to 12 hours.

BROCCOLI WITH LEMON SAUCE

  2 pkgs. (10 oz. each)
    frozen broccoli spears
  ½ cup slivered almonds
  1 tablespoon butter or
    margarine
  2 pkg. (3 oz. each) cream
    cheese
  ⅓ cup milk
  1 teaspoon grated lemon
    peel
  1 teaspoon lemon juice
  ½ teaspoon ground ginger
  ¼ teaspoon salt

Cook broccoli as directed on package. In fry pan, cook almonds in butter until golden brown. Remove almonds and set aside. Add cream cheese, milk, lemon peel and juice, ginger and salt. Heat until smooth and creamy. Pour over broccoli. Garnish with almonds.

6 to 8 servings

DOUBLE CORN SCALLOP

  2 eggs, well beaten
  1 cup milk
  17-oz. can cream-style corn
  7-oz. can whole kernel
    corn with sweet
    peppers, drained
  ¾ cup (20 crackers) coarse
    saltine cracker crumbs
  ¼ cup finely chopped
    onion
  1 tablespoon finely
    chopped green pepper
  ¾ teaspoon salt
  ⅛ teaspoon pepper
  2 tablespoons butter or
    margarine, melted
  ½ cup (13 crackers) fine
    saltine cracker crumbs

In bowl, combine all ingredients except butter and ½ cup cracker crumbs. Turn into greased 1½-quart or 10x6-inch baking dish. Toss ½ cup cracker crumbs with melted butter; sprinkle over corn mixture. Bake at 350°F. for 35 to 45 minutes until knife inserted in center comes out clean.

6 to 8 servings

This refreshing salad tempter is the perfect color for your holiday table.

DAIQUIRI FRUIT SALAD

  1½ cups (15¼-oz. can)
    crushed pineapple
  3-oz. pkg. lime or
    lemon-flavored gelatin
  ½ cup frozen limeade
    concentrate, thawed
  ⅓ cup salad dressing or
    mayonnaise
  2 cups whipped topping
    or whipped cream
  2 medium bananas, sliced

Drain pineapple, reserving syrup. Add water to syrup to make 1 cup. Bring to a boil; add gelatin and stir to dissolve. Add frozen limeade concentrate and salad dressing; stir until well blended. Chill until slightly thickened but not set, about 45 minutes. Fold in pineapple and remaining ingredients. Pour into 1½-quart ring mold or 8-inch square pan. Freeze until firm, about 4 hours. To serve, unmold or cut into squares.

5 to 6 servings

TIP: Salad can be refrigerated as well as frozen. If desired, add ½ cup chopped nuts with pineapple.

A versatile pudding which can be steamed or baked in the oven.

STEAMED CHRISTMAS PUDDING

    1 cup Pillsbury's Best All Purpose or Unbleached Flour
    3 tablespoons brown sugar
    ½ teaspoon baking powder
    ¼ teaspoon soda
    ½ teaspoon salt
    ½ teaspoon cinnamon
    ⅛ teaspoon nutmeg
    ⅛ teaspoon ground ginger
       Dash ground cloves
    3 tablespoons cooking oil
    ½ cup raisins or chopped dates
    ¼ cup chopped nuts
    ½ cup milk
    3 tablespoons molasses

In bowl, combine all ingredients. Mix until dry ingredients are moistened. Spoon into well-greased (not oiled) 1-quart mold or casserole or 6-cup fluted tube pan. Cover with lid or foil. Place on rack in large steamer or kettle. Pour boiling water into steamer until 2 inches deep; cover.* Reduce heat to low. Steam 1½ to 2 hours until pudding springs back when lightly touched in center. Cut in slices. Serve hot, with Hard, Lemon or Nutmeg Sauce.

6 to 8 servings

TIP: *If desired, cover and bake in 325°F. oven for 55 to 60 minutes until top springs back when lightly touched in center.

LEMON SAUCE

    ½ cup sugar
    2 tablespoons cornstarch
       Dash salt
    1 cup hot water
    2 teaspoons grated lemon peel
    2 tablespoons lemon juice
    2 tablespoons butter or margarine

In saucepan, combine sugar, cornstarch and salt; blend in water. Cook over medium heat, stirring constantly, until mixture boils 1 minute and is clear and slightly thickened. Remove from heat. Stir in lemon peel, juice and butter. Serve warm or cool on steamed pudding.

1½ cups

TIP: For Orange Sauce, substitute orange juice for water and orange peel for lemon peel; omit lemon juice.

NUTMEG SAUCE

    ½ cup sugar
    1 tablespoon cornstarch
    ½ teaspoon nutmeg
    1 cup water or milk
    ¼ cup butter or margarine
    1 teaspoon vanilla or 1 tablespoon rum or brandy

In saucepan, combine sugar, cornstarch and nutmeg. Stir in water and butter. Cook over medium heat until mixture boils 1 minute and is slightly thickened. Add vanilla. Serve warm over steamed pudding.

1⅓ cups

HARD SAUCE

    1 cup powdered sugar
    ¼ cup butter or margarine, softened
    1 teaspoon rum or brandy flavoring or 1 tablespoon rum or brandy
    ½ teaspoon vanilla
       Dash salt

In small bowl, combine all ingredients until smooth and creamy. (Add 1 to 2 teaspoons water if necessary.) Beat at high speed until fluffy. Chill until served. Serve on warm steamed pudding.

1 cup

Cranberry-Stuffed Pork Crown Roast, p. 135

Index